Peterbald Cats

Peterbald Cats Owner's Manual.

Peterbald cats care, personality, grooming, health and feeding all included.

by

Harvey Hendisson

ALL RIGHTS RESERVED. This book contains material protected under International and Federal Copyright Laws and Treaties.

Any unauthorized reprint or use of this material is strictly prohibited. No part of this book may be reproduced or transmitted in any form or by any means, electronic, mechanical or otherwise, including photocopying or recording, or by any information storage and retrieval system without express written permission from the author.

Copyrighted © 2014

Published by: IMB Publishing

Table of Contents

Table of Contents 3

Chapter 1: Introduction 7

Chapter 2: The history of the Peterbald Cat 8

    1) The history and origin of the Peterbald cat 8

    2) The status of the breed 8

Chapter 3: General information about the Peterbald 9

    1) The Peterbald versus the Sphynx 9

    2) Peterbald Breeding Standards 10

    3) Common myths 11

    4) Life span 13

    5) Intelligence 13

    6) How often to play with your Peterbald 14

    7) The amount of space they need 14

    8) Indoor versus outdoor cats 15

    9) The Peterbald cat's temperament 19

    10) The Peterbald anatomy 20

Chapter 4: Before you buy your Peterbald 21

    1) Questions to ask before bringing a Peterbald home 21

    2) The shopping list for your new kitten or cat 22

    3) Removing household hazards 24

Chapter 5: Choosing your Peterbald 28

Table of Contents

1) General considerations 29

2) What to ask the breeder 30

Chapter 6: Your new Peterbald kitten or cat 32

1) The first important few hours 32

2) Settling in 32

3) Bringing home an adult Peterbald 34

4) Preparing your family for a pet 35

5) Make time for your new cat 36

6) Complicated scenarios 37

7) Training 41

8) How long a Peterbald can be left alone 48

9) Transporting your Peterbald 48

10) Keeping your Peterbald warm 49

11) To microchip your cat or not 49

Chapter 7: Feeding your Peterbald 51

1) What to feed your kitten and how often 51

2) What to feed adult cats and how often 51

3) What not to feed your Peterbald cat 56

4) Treats 57

Chapter 8: Grooming your Peterbald 59

1) Bathing your Peterbald 59

2) Eye and face care 60

3) Nail care and clipping 60

4) Ear care 60

5) Tooth care 61

Table of Contents

6) Products to use 61

Chapter 9: Your Peterbald's health 62

1) Finding a good vet 62
2) Preparing your Cat for a vet visit 64
3) Vaccinations 68
4) Neutering and spaying 69
5) General early signs of illness 71
6) Common cat illnesses and health problems 72
7) More serious conditions 77
8) Obesity in Peterbald cats 87
9) How to give your Peterbald medication 92
10) How to clean your cat's teeth 93
11) The self-medicating cat 95
12) De-clawing a cat 95
13) A first aid kit for your cat 98
14) Preparing your cat for surgery 99
15) The recovery process 99

Chapter 10: Behavioural issues 101

1) Sleeping habits 101
2) Behaviour problems 102
3) Going away and travelling with your Peterbald 106
4) Why and how your cat purrs 111
5) Feline stress and dealing with it 111
6) Moving house with your cat 113

Chapter 11: Becoming a Peterbald breeder 115

Table of Contents

1) Sexual maturity 116

2) Breeding: general pointers 116

3) Finding the right mate 117

4) What to feed your pregnant cat 118

5) Gestation 119

6) Special care for a pregnant cat 120

7) Preparing for and assisting at the birth 121

8) The birth itself 122

9) Dealing with the umbilical cord if the mother doesn't 123

10) Feeding kittens if the mother can't or shouldn't 124

Chapter 12: The aging Peterbald cat 125

1) The aging Peterbald 125

2) How to make your aging Peterbald more comfortable 127

3) How do you know it's time to let go? 127

Chapter 13: Prices and costs 129

1) How to choose a breeder 129

2) The cost to purchase a Peterbald cat or kitten 130

3) Monthly costs of caring for your cat 130

4) The option to take out Pet Insurance 131

Chapter 14: General advice & tips 133

Conclusion 136

Chapter 1: Introduction

The Peterbald, originating in Russian in the late 1990's, is a very new breed that has already received recognition from many cat associations and registries and has gained a strong and devoted following amongst cat lovers.

These are extremely elegant medium-sized cats with a slim, graceful yet muscular build. Some Peterbalds are hairless but others have a velour, or flocked or a brush coat. The pigmentation and coat variations are huge and lovely.

This breed is very sweet-natured, affectionate, chatty, energetic and loving. They are highly intelligent and sociable cats who will follow their owners around just so they can be near them. The Peterbald gets on well with other cats and cat-friendly dogs. They are also very good with children.

However, these cats do need a great deal of time and energy as they require regular grooming including bathing, lots of cuddles and petting and plenty of play time. They do not do well if they are left alone often and for extended periods as they will become unhappy and stressed.

Finally, please note that some of the information in this book is not specific to the Peterbald but can be applied to all cats. However, much of the details and tips are breed specific. I hope you find this book useful and fun to read.

Chapter 2: The history of the Peterbald Cat

1) The history and origin of the Peterbald cat

The Peterbald is a very new breed compared to many others as it was only created in 1994. In 1993, or 1988 according to some sources, a cat breeder by the name of Olga S. Mironova crossed a brown mackerel tabby Don Hairless – also known as a Donskoy or Donsky – called *Afinguen Myth* with a tortoiseshell Oriental Shorthair called *Radma Vom Jagerhof*.

The result of the first two letters were four hairless oriental kittens: *Muscat iz Murino*, *Nezhenka iz Murino*, *Mandarin iz Murino* and *Nocturne iz Murino*. These cats formed the foundation of a new breed: the Peterbald. The breed's name was supposedly derived from the fact that it originated in St. Petersburg in Russia.

The Peterbald breeding program later added Siamese and Russian Blues in order to widen and strengthen the genetic pool. Current permissible outcrosses for the breed are the Siamese, Oriental Shorthair and the Don Hairless (Don Sphynx). The Balinese and Javanese were ruled to be unacceptable in 2005.

2) The status of the breed

The Peterbald was recognised by The International Cat Association (TICA) in 1997 in the Preliminary New Breed category and achieved Championship breed status in 2005. 2008 saw the brush coat Peterbald recognised in the Championship category. The World Cat Federation (WCF) accepted the breed in 2003 and the American Cat Fanciers Association (ACFA) followed suite in 2009.

However, there are still some cat associations and registries that do not recognize the breed due to health concerns.

Chapter 3: General information about the Peterbald

1) The Peterbald versus the Sphynx

Some people look at the Peterbald and the Sphynx and, based on the fact that they are both hairless, assume they are the same breed. This is far from the case. There are several significant differences.

Firstly, the Peterbald's hairlessness or hair loss is the result of a dominant gene. The Sphynx is hairless thanks to a recessive gene. It is also important to note that the Sphynx gene is for complete hairlessness whereas the Peterbald's gene is for hair loss!

There are also marked differences in terms of the overall appearance of the two breeds:

- Sphynx cats feel like warm peaches or chamois. Peterbalds can have a variety of coats from entirely bald to a brush coat.
- The Peterbald has a long, elongated face whereas the Sphynx has a much shorter, wider face.
- The body type of the Peterbald is refined and elegant. The Sphynx, on the other hand, is a medium sized cat that is more pear-shaped and has a round tummy.
- Peterbald's eyes are almost almond shaped eyes. The Sphynx has lemon-shaped eyes.
- The boning of a Peterbald is medium-fine whereas the Sphynx is medium boned.
- The ears are set lower on the Peterbald than on a Sphynx.
- Many Peterbald have kinked whiskers, but the Sphynx cat usually has broken or no whiskers.

Chapter 3: General information about the Peterbald

2) Peterbald Breeding Standards

The standards governing the Peterbald when it comes to judging are determined by TICA and apply to each aspect of the cat.

- *Head*: A long inverted triangle with a strong, blunted chin. The forehead should be flat and the profile almost straight.
- *Ears*: Extra large, slightly flared, broad at the base and pointed.
- *Eyes*: Medium-sized, flush with the skull / not protruding or set back in the skull, almost almond-shaped and an eye's width between the eyes.
- *Muzzle*: Slightly blunt, strong, smooth and there should be kinky whiskers.
- *Neck*: Slender and long.
- *Torso*: Medium-sized, graceful and long. The width of the hips and shoulders should be the same.
- *Legs*: Forelegs must be vertical and straight. Hind legs are slightly longer. Bones are medium-fine and long. Limbs are well muscled and strong.
- *Feet*: Medium sized and oval in shape. The toes are both prominent and agile. The foot pads, however, are not prominent.
- *Tail*: Thin or whippy, long and strongly muscled.
- *Coat*: Three coats are found in the breed and all are accepted in terms of the standards. The three are hairless, flocked or velour and a brush coat.

Some Peterbalds are born hairless. Others are born with hair which they loose over time. The hairless Peterbald feels soft, warm and almost sticky to the touch. Perhaps the best description, also used of the Sphynx, is that it feels like warm chamois. The hairless Peterbalds can have pronounced wrinkles all over the face, body and feet.

Peterbalds with the flocked or velour coat have anything from sparse and fine downy hair to slightly longer, closer down. This coat feels more like suede or even crushed velvet. Cats with a velour or flocked coat often appear hairless from a distance. In summary, a velour cat is about 70% hairless and a flock cat is approximately 90% hairless.

No other breed has a coat like the Peterbald's brush coat. It is a wiry and dense coat that is irregular in both texture and length. There are parts of the coat that feel soft and other more curly sections that are coarse to the touch. Regardless of the type and length of coat you should always be able to see the cat's skin through the hair.

Some Peterbalds have combination coats: a flocked or velour body and short, downy brush coat on the extremities. Most Peterbald owners are not concerned about all of the breed standard requirements. However, they must be referred to by those who judge cats at association championships and by breeders who wish to select an ideal cat for this purpose.

3) Common myths

There are a number of popular myths about the Peterbald that need to be exploded.

Chapter 3: General information about the Peterbald

Hairless cats don't need to be groomed

It is thought by some that hairless, or near hairless, cats don't need to be groomed because there is no or little fur that could get dirty or matted. Acting according to this misapprehension will have negative consequences for both a Peterbald and his or her owner.

It is the hairlessness that in fact makes it so important to groom these cats regularly and carefully. Because there is no or minimal fur to absorb the normal skin oils these cats need to be washed and bathed regularly. If not they develop infections and other skin problems… and they can leave oily marks on furniture or your clothes. In addition, a hairless inner ear means that dirt can't be filtered out as it is in a furry ear. This can lead to health problems.

Peterbald cats are particularly prone to illness

The next piece of misinformation is that Peterbald are especially prone to illness. They are no more so than any other breed and are generally robust cats.

There are, however, a few routine issues an owner must be aware of. Given the lack of coat or thick coat these cats are certainly more vulnerable to the sun. As a result their exposure should be limited as they can get sunburnt or, worst case scenario, develop skin cancer in later life. This is especially true of cats with light pigmentation in their skins. Peterbalds are also susceptible to the cold and need to be kept warm. Finally, unless they are washed and bathed regularly they can get skin, eye and ear infections because of the lack of hair.

While they are generally healthy, they do carry the risk of Feline ectodermal dysplasia. This condition, thought to be linked to gene that causes hairlessness or hair loss, causes dental problems such as malformed or missing teeth and lactation issues which is a problem if the cat has kittens to feed.

Chapter 3: General information about the Peterbald

Peterbald cats are hypoallergenic

Because they are hairless or nearly so, some people believe that Peterbald cats are hypoallergenic. This is not the case.

Allergies in humans are caused either by feline dander or the Fel d1 protein. Dander is the name given to the mixture of dead skin cells, hair and skin oils that all cats produce. Fel d1 protein is primarily found in sebaceous oils and saliva. While the Peterbald will produce far less dander because it is hairless, or virtually so, there will still be some. All cats lick themselves so if this sticky protein is the primary cause of allergy. Not much can be done to avoid the protein or dander other than bathing the cat regularly.

4) Life span

Because this is a relatively new breed it is more difficult to give an average or even an accurate range. However, based on the longevity of the Oriental and Don Sphynx many breeders believe that a well cared for Peterbald will have a life expectancy of about 12 - 15 years.

5) Intelligence

No matter what source one consults, one of the constants is the view that the Peterbald is one of the most intelligent of cat breeds. This means they need a great deal of interaction and stimulation either from their owner or from another cat… preferably both!

As a result of their natural curiosity and intelligence, they are easy to train. That is, they are as easy to train as they – or any other cat – want to be. Peterbalds can be taught to sit, to walk on a lead or leash, use a toilet and even respond to some voice commands. They also have elegant oval paws with which they can pick objects up and grasp them. These objects include door knobs!

Like any other breed the Peterbald requires mental stimulation. You can keep your cat mentally active by giving it puzzles and toys. You will be surprised by how eager your cat will be to solve and complete puzzles successfully.

Curiosity is a quality that is common in the Peterbald. You will see your cat prodding at objects or poking around your home. They will also be very curious about you. They want to know what you are doing, where you are going etc. You will notice your kitty walking around you with, enquiring about your day by simply staring at you. They will also sit on high shelves and simply watch over the household.

Their intelligence combined with their long toes mean that they will acquire skills like opening the door and getting their toys out when they want them. Unfortunately they are not usually satisfied with just one toy. They need a several toys to stimulate their minds.

6) *How often to play with your Peterbald*

The answer to this question is, "As often as you can!" These charming cats are gregarious, energetic, highly sociable and acrobatic and they enjoy your company and getting attention immensely. In fact, being the centre of attention is his or her ambition. In addition, they seem to go out of their way to make play time as fun for you as it is for them. The Peterbald that gets attention and playtime will be a very happy, loving and relaxed cat because they are by nature extremely active cats and love playing. They also love to be in your company.

Watching your Peterbald is extremely entertaining as they can be real clowns and they are very acrobatic. They are also a chatty or talkative breed.

7) *The amount of space they need*

These cats do not require a lot of space. They are also, preferably, indoor cats because they are more vulnerable to the sun and potential rashes caused by contact with plants, grasses etc.

Chapter 3: General information about the Peterbald

This makes Peterbald the ideal cats to have regardless of whether you live in an apartment or a house and do or don't have a garden. As long as there is enough space for them to play, jump and run around they will be fit and contented.

So, a garden or outdoor space is not essential if you have a Peterbald. Their standard levels of energy, curiosity and playfulness mean that it takes very little prompting or encouragement from their owner to get them to exercise.

Games that involve running to chase an object such as a ball or a piece of string being pulled along to floor, or jumping up to swat at or catch a toy, will give your cat loads of healthy exercise and be a huge amount of fun for you both. If you have more than one cat they will play games together.

8) Indoor versus outdoor cats

It is fairly commonly thought that it is impossible, even cruel, to confine a cat indoors. This is rarely the case but certainly not applicable to a breed like the Peterbald where the cat is focused on you, its owner, rather than the space it inhabits. It will be happy and more than content to be inside and with you.

If you aren't there, a comfortable, warm place to sleep, food and a companion and toys are all your cat needs to have a day that is full of all it needs to stay healthy and stimulated. There are numerous reasons why having an indoor cat is in fact preferable.

Firstly, skin cancer is a problem with most cat breeds. However, cats with white fur and hairless cats are of course far more at risk. If you live in a country or a part of the world where the weather and UV conditions mean that skin cancer is highly prevalent, you must take steps to protect your cat from exposure to sunlight.

Your Peterbald can of course have some exposure to sun. In fact, lying in a patch of sun is a favourite way to keep warm. Owners should make sure, though, that if a cat is left in a sunny space –

Chapter 3: General information about the Peterbald

especially an enclosed one like a courtyard – that there is access to shaded places so that he or she can cool down and doesn't get burnt.

Also, hairless cats are of course more susceptible to fluctuations in temperature. Although the Peterbald has a higher than average body temperature they still feel the cold far more than cats that have hair or fur. It stands to reason that a 'naked' or thinly 'dressed' cat will get very chilly compared to one in a fur coat.

While adults are better able to regulate their body temperatures and either look for and move to a warm or cool area, kittens are not able to do either. They can overheat and get dangerously cold very quickly; this often leads to serious respiratory problems.

Thirdly, outdoor cats – especially those that roam – are far more at risk of picking up infections from the other cats they may come into contact with. Not all cats will be up to date with vaccinations or as healthy as they could be and your cat might cross paths with an infected animal. No cat owner wants to exposure their cat to the danger of contracting Feline Immunodeficiency Virus or Feline Leukemia both of which are quite common in cats that roam outside, are easily transmitted and fatal for cats.

In addition to the risk of infection is the danger of injuries as a result of fights with other cats including strays or even feral cats. Some bites can lead to abscesses which can make a cat really sick very fast. Other illnesses such as rabies can be passed on by a bite or scratch from an infected cat.

Other cats are not the only animals that pose a potential threat to your Peterbald. Domesticated cats that wander from their home are usually not able to defend themselves against animals like dogs, opossums, foxes and snakes. These encounters will often result in serious injuries or even death immediately or some time later as a result of infection. If your cat wanders into the wrong areas it becomes vulnerable to attacks from any of these creatures that are defending a territory or acting from fear or aggression.

Chapter 3: General information about the Peterbald

The other potentially dangerous creatures out there are people who have been known to injure or kill cats.

Cats that roam around outside are also inevitably going to encounter a further danger: roads and traffic. Although many cats are smart enough to avoid the sound of approaching vehicles, a cat might run across a road if frightened by something such as a dog or a loud noise. In most cases an encounter with a motor car will result in very serious injury or death.

Threats to your cat also come in the form of parasites such as fleas and ticks and fungi such as ringworm. Undergrowth, sand and stray or untreated cats harbour ticks and fleas. Both of these insects could potentially get onto your Peterbald. Admittedly it is easier to spot them on a hairless cat, and the lack of hair might make the Peterbald less appealing to fleas. However, fleas carry diseases that can potentially make your cat and you unwell.

Ticks are even more dangerous as certain types can paralyze or even kill a cat if not treated correctly. Tick bites for humans can cause serious illness too. A cat that wanders around outdoors could also pick up ringworm which is easily transmitted to people. This is not a serious or life threatening problem but it is not easy to treat and tends to recur as a result.

A further danger facing an outdoor cat is getting lost. A cat can get distracted by an interesting scent, chase after a small animal or another cat and then loose its bearings. It's best not to even dwell on the possibility that your valuable Peterbald could get stolen... but it could happen. Even individuals who don't realise the value of a cat may take it because they like it, think it's a stray or to use for appalling things like religious practices or even to sell to a laboratory that does testing on animals. While the chance of these horrors is small, why take the risk?

Keeping a cat indoors also reduces the potential for disputes with neighbours and ill-feeling. A cat might decide that a flower bed next door makes the ideal outdoor litter box. While performing

Chapter 3: General information about the Peterbald

the necessary excavations, plants might be uprooted or damaged. Even if there's no damage your neighbour is unlikely to be charmed with the new type of manure being deposited in her or his garden by your cat! There's also the possibility that your cat could get into a fight with a neighbourhood cat; you might be expected to pay the resulting vet bills. Finally, your male cat might not be popular if he impregnates the cat next door.

Keep in mind that the most important thing in your cat's life will be you. This means that your Peterbald cat, whether male or female, will be more than happy to be a home body if you are there and if he or she has some company, or at least a few toys, and enough food and water when you are out. Given they are very intelligent and curious these cats are unlikely to get bored and playing with them will give them enough exercise and stimulation to keep them fit physically and emotionally.

Given all of these factors in favour of keeping your cat inside it is hardly surprising to learn that indoor cats have much healthier and longer lives that their outdoor counterparts. If you are reluctant, however, to keep your cat inside but don't want your Peterbald to roam there is the option of building a cat enclosure.

A cat enclosure is much more than a cage. Regardless of the amount of space you have available outside, you can create of really fun and safe outdoor area for your Peterbald. It will of course have to be enclosed and you need to use cat proof fences. The height of a fence is a consideration too as a cat can leap five times its own height from a standing position!

You could either build an enclosure yourself or purchase one. If you have a significant amount of space – and a fair bit of money – available, a cat enclosure can be large enough to include ramps, sleeping platforms, tunnels for play, tree branches and so on. Remember that it is essential that there are both warm and shaded spots so your Peterbald does not get either cold or sun burnt.

An alternative, if you have less space, is a cat run. This could be an enclosed narrow strip down the side of a house or an enclosed veranda or balcony. With a smaller space such as a balcony you could use cat netting. Again, the addition of things to climb up, onto or through will make it a fun and stimulating place for your cat.

Regardless of whether you have an enclosure or run for your Peterbald, you must make sure that it has easy and safe access to it through a window or cat flap. If the enclosure is some distance from the house, you could consider an enclosed tunnel from the point of exit to the enclosure. This way your cat has exercise just getting to and from its outdoor enclosure!

9) *The Peterbald cat's temperament*

There seems to be general consensus with regards to the temperament or personality of the Peterbald.

These cats are described as intelligent, inquisitive, entertaining, clownish, gentle and sweet-tempered, outgoing, acrobatic, quick, friendly, energetic, demonstrative and cuddly, loving, sociable, bold, affectionate, playful, mischievous, companionable, devoted, sweet-tempered, active, attention-seeking, chatty, adventurous, loyal, cheeky, comical and flirtatious. In fact, most sources place "extremely" or "incredibly", or at the very least "very", in front of each of those.

They enjoy the company of other cats and of cat-friendly dogs and will be friendly to your guests. However, they adore the companionship of their special person and will follow him or her around and are always ready for a chat, a cuddle or a game.

Some Peterbald fans have gone so far as to say that this breed is the most dog-like of all the cat breeds. Some cat people would say that is no complement, but let's look at why. Firstly, the Peterbald is the most easily trained cat breed. They can even be taught to walk on a leash and are happy to go on fairly long walks if accompanied by their owner.

In addition to going for walks, a Peterbald will learn to play fetch and do tricks that it finds fun and that it realises you enjoy, and it will respond to certain voice commands. Just like dogs, and some cats, the Peterbald is very loyal and owner rather than place or territory orientated. This makes moving house much easier.

Furthermore, there is nothing stand-offish about these cats; they thrive on being loved and showing their love. So, if you want a quiet, aloof, independent and docile cat, don't get a Peterbald!

10) The Peterbald anatomy

Average adult size and weight

The Peterbald is a medium sized, well-muscled and long-boned cat. As a rule, female Peterbald cats weigh 6 - 8 lbs (3 - 4 kg) and male cats weigh 8 - 10 lbs (4 – 4.5 kg).

The Peterbald usually require a slightly higher caloric intake than other breeds because they have a very high metabolism and their bodies have to work hard all the time to keep their body warm. However, these cats are very fond of their food and tend to gain weight unless they are given a calorie controlled diet.

Pigmentation and colours

Pigment cells are responsible for the colour in the Peterbald's skin and eyes. In terms of the skin and any coat present, these cats are found in a wide range of colours. One gets pure white cats, solid colour such as black, pointed, tabby and even tortoiseshell. Interestingly, eyes without pigment cells are blue. Polygenes that influence eye colour can be manipulated by breeders who wish to produce cats with bicoloured or odd eyes. There are even instances of asymmetrical bicoloured eyes. However, many Peterbald cats have blue eyes.

Chapter 4: Before you buy your Peterbald

1) Questions to ask before bringing a Peterbald home

The first issue you need to consider before buying a Peterbald, or any other pet for that matter, is whether you are prepared and able to be a responsible owner.

As previously indicated, this particular breed will need your time and your love. The grooming care that he will she will require is significant so unless you are prepared to do all that is necessary to keep your cat happy and healthy don't get a Peterbald.

There are several lifestyle factors that a potential Peterbald owner must consider:

1. **Time**: more than with any other cat, a Peterbald kitten or cat will require a great deal of time whether it is in order to groom them, play with them or simply to spend time with them. Also, does your work or social life take you away from home a great deal? If it does this will pose a problem as Peterbald cats are not good at being left alone either frequently or for long periods.
2. **Environment**: is your living space sufficiently large to accommodate a very active cat? Are there things in your environment which pose a danger to an animal? If there are any hazards in the environment, are you able to easily remove them?
3. **Cost**: the first significant cost is, of course, the price you will have to pay for the Peterbald kitten or cat that you choose. Thereafter there will be regular expenses including food, vet or medical expenses, grooming products and other incidentals such as bedding, toys, scratching post et cetera.

4. **Patience**: because Peterbald kittens and cats are so very active, adjusting to them can be a little difficult initially. In addition, while the litter box training is fairly quick, toilet training your cat will take a lot longer. Finally, as with any boisterous small animal your kitten may knock over and break items. In fact, there can be breakages with adult cats too because of their energy and activity levels.
5. **A thick skin**: as the owner of a Peterbald you will probably receive a number of strange or rude reactions and comments about your cat from family and friends. Many owners also have to deal with some pretty silly questions from people who behave as though the Peterbald is not a cat!

2) The shopping list for your new kitten or cat

There are several items that should, preferably, be acquired before you fetch your Peterbald and bring your new companion home.

Food and related items

The first item is food. Obviously the type of food you purchase will depend of whether you are going to bring a kitten or a cat home because different age cats have differing nutritional needs. It is recommended that you purchase a mixture of canned food and dry food. Like people, cats enjoy a varied diet. On the can or the bag of food it will clearly state the age of the cat that the food has been formulated for.

Some Peterbald owners are great supporters of a diet of bones and raw food for their cats. However, this is not recommended with very young cats. It also may not supply all the vitamins that your cat requires.

In addition to the food itself, you will need to purchase food and water bowls. It's always a good idea to have more than one per cat so that you can insure that you have a clean bowl to use at all times.

Because the Peterbald has a very high metabolism and needs to generate a lot of heat they require frequent small meals. As you are not going to be with your cat all the time, it can be a very good idea to purchase an automatic food dispenser. This way your cat will not be without food at any stage during the day or night.

Cat Litter

There is a vast array of cat litters available commercially. The general rule of thumb is to avoid scented litters; while you might prefer them it's highly unlikely that your cat with its highly developed sense of smell will. Cat litters that clump are also to be avoided, especially if you have a young cat that might eat some of the litter and subsequently suffer from blockages in the digestive system.

Working out what the best litter is for your cat is a question of trial and error. Eventually you will find the one that your cat responds to best and that you don't find too onerous to clean or replace. If you ever run out of clean cat litter an emergency measure that works very effectively is either soil or sand from your garden or shredded newspaper.

Bed and bedding

While it's not always necessary to buy a bed and bedding for a cat it can be a good idea to do so for a Peterbald, particularly if you live in a cold climate or your home is cool. The igloo style bed retains heat better than an open basket.

Of course, given you are dealing with a cat you could buy a bed that will be ignored in favour of a couch, a chair or under the covers on your bed!

Toys

There is also a wide range of toys available for cats and kittens that vary in sophistication and cost. You could certainly choose one or two of these to have at your home for when your new charge arrives.

Alternatively, it is not always necessary to buy toys as one can make them. For example, a kitten or cat will have hours of enjoyment chasing the end of a piece of string, jumping up to catch a cork or a small ball suspended by piece of string. It is perhaps better to get to know your cat a little before deciding what sort of toys he or she is likely to respond to best.

Scratching post

It's not only important for your cat to have a scratching post to keep their claws sharp, you and your furniture need this piece of equipment too because your cat is far less likely to sharpen its claws on your furniture if it has a post.

A scratching post is necessary to help keep your cat's claws healthy too. And it's another item for your Peterbald to play with…

Clothing

Opinion is divided about clothing for Peterbald cats and, in fact, cats in general. Some owners believe that it is necessary to keep these cats warm because they feel the cold more than most.

On the other hand there are Peterbald owners who believe that clothing is unnatural on a cat and it just causes the animal stress and, in the worst case scenario, an adverse skin reaction in cats that have little or no hair.

3) Removing household hazards

Medicine

One of the most toxic substances for a cat is your prescription medications or drugs. They are in fact the most common cause of poisoning in cats. For instance, an ingredient like ibuprofen which is found in many painkillers is deadly for cats.

Just as you would for children, you must ensure that all drugs or medications are kept where your cat cannot find them and ingest them.

Electrical appliances

While it is not always possible to remove electrical appliances or their cords, one needs to take care with them because kittens and young cats especially like playing with moving or dangling objects. An electrical cord attached to an iron, for example, will be almost irresistible to a young kitten or young-at-heart cat like a Peterbald. He or she will pull on the cord or swing from it.

This could be very dangerous for both the cat and your property. In addition, if the cat's teeth penetrate the cord's plastic covering he or she will receive an electric shock.

Poisons

Cats are foragers by nature. Peterbald cats are especially curious and adventurous. It's very important that you don't leave any garden pest powders, pellets and sprays; weed killers; cleaning materials; contaminated foods or foods toxic to cats exposed and accessible. If you do, your cat will find them and, although they are not indiscriminate, there is a chance that they will eat poison.

Poisonous plants

There are certain plants we might have either in a garden or as indoor or potted plants that are poisonous or potentially deadly for cats. In fact, the list of plants toxic to cats is astonishingly lengthy. It includes Rhododendrons and Azaleas, Lily-of-the-Valley, the lily family, Amaryllis, Holly, Asparagus Fern, Begonia, Clivia, Chrysanthemums and Cycads to name just a few.

It is unlikely that your Peterbald will decide to snack on one of these. However, the likelihood increases slightly with an indoor cat. You will have to decide how great a risk the plants you have pose. Generally speaking you should avoid plants with variegated leaves.

Swimming pools

If you have a swimming pool a secure pool cover is a good idea while your cat is young. Don't ever leave a kitten near a pool or even a pond unattended. If your neighbour has a pool or pond there's not much you can do about it.

However, once your cat is settled, you can and should teach it about pool safety (see the relevant section of "Training" in chapter 6).

Doors and windows

When you bring your new kitten, or more especially your new cat, home for the first time, you must see that all the windows and external doors are closed.

The Peterbald is a stay-at-home cat by nature but any cat that is confronted by new sights, sounds, smells and people may feel overwhelmed, panic and dash about initially. The last thing you want is for a frightened cat to vanish through an open door and window!

Heat sources

The Peterbald, because it is hairless or almost so and feels the colds far more than other breeds, is particularly attracted to sources of heat. Some of these are dangerous for a cat to be around. You need to take precautions to prevent your cat becoming burnt.

You need to be careful with stoves, stove hot plates, heaters, exposed light bulbs, fireplaces and the inside of large appliances such as dish washers and tumble dryers that may be warm. Your cat may cosy up to or in any one of these and not realize till it's too late that its delicate skin has been affected. These cats also seek out the sun and can end up sunburned so you need to intervene.

Try to screen open or accessible heat sources within the home and close appliances such as tumble dryers so your cat can't climb in. If he or she has outside time you can ensure that it does not last too long and your cat does not get overheated or sun burnt.

Chapter 5: Choosing your Peterbald

Choosing the Peterbald that is going to become your companion is both important and difficult. This is especially the case if you are confronted by a number of kittens, each with its own personality and characteristics. Selecting a kitten using the, "Ooh! That one is *so* cute!" method is not good enough. You must take your time to find the kitten that is right for you.

While much of your decision will be based on the kitten or cat itself, if you are getting a kitten from a breeder then he or she will also affect your choice. If the breeder has socialized the kittens they will be happy – or at least comfortable – to be picked up and handled. If the kittens aren't and seem fearful of people or nervous this is an indication that the kittens have not been well treated and may exhibit behavioural problems now and / or later in life.

You also need to assess the kitten or cat's state of health. Have a careful look at the eyes which should be clear and bright. Make sure that there is no discharge from its eyes, ears or nose. The gums and tongue should be pink. The skin of a hairless kitten or cat should not feel dry or oily. Watch that the kitten's gait is even. Ensure that it has good hearing and eyesight by making a noise and moving your finger. If the kitten turns to the sound and follows the movement it means its sight and hearing are fine.

After you have looked at health and general behaviour you can sit back and watch the kittens play and interact, look at markings and eye colour if that is important to you, and consider things such as personality, energy levels and curiosity.

It is worth taking your time to choose the kitten that will be right for you. The wrong choice may result in having to return the kitten which will be upsetting for you and traumatic for the kitten.

1) General considerations

Getting one or two cats

As stated previously, Peterbald cats are extremely sociable and loving. They adore company and need affection. If you are away from home each day, to go to work for example, then it is a good idea to get two cats.

They will be play companions and can curl up and sleep together in your absence. They will also provide moral support to each other when they confront a new situation.

Buying a male or female

This is a hotly debated question and it can be an important consideration. Some believe that male and female cats are cast in similar stereotypical moulds as their human counterparts: males are more physical, even aggressive, and females are gentler.

However, other cat owners – me included – have had experiences that prove the opposite: gentle, stay-at-home (neutered) males and females prone to bouts of ill temper and sulking. Many believe that one should choose a kitten or cat based on health and personality; don't let gender be the deciding factor.

Chapter 5: Choosing your Peterbald

The age a kitten should be when you buy it

A reputable breeder won't allow anyone to take a kitten that is younger than 12 weeks old. Under this age Peterbald kittens are prone to respiratory infections. They need time to get strong and to have the required vaccinations and deworming.

A registered versus a non-registered kitten

If you obtain a kitten from a registered and reputable breeder, a registered kitten comes with a number of advantages.

Firstly, you know that your Peterbald kitten is actually a pure Peterbald. Secondly, you can rest assured that the kitten is old enough to leave its mother and it has been socialized. In addition, a registered cat is far less likely to carry genetic or other illnesses. The breeder will also have had the necessary vaccinations done and the kitten will be dewormed.

With an unregistered kitten you have none of these assurances; there's no guarantee the kitten is either healthy or even a Peterbald.

2) What to ask the breeder

When you talk to breeders, either when you are selecting one or before choosing your Peterbald, there are a number of issues you need to discuss and investigate.

The breeder and the facility

To begin with, you want to know about the breeder and the facility. You need to ask to see proof of his or her registration as a Peterbald breeder.

A tour of the breeder's premises is also recommended. Where are the cats housed? Are the rooms, runs or areas the cats are in clean, airy and spacious? If a breeder refuses to let you look around, leave!

The kitten or cat's lineage and the breeding pair

You should ask the breeder about the kitten's lineage, including the age of the mother and father because cats should not be bred past the age of 4 or 5. You also want assurances, and preferably proof, of the health of the breeding pair in terms of vaccinations and overall health. If you intend to show your cat you should also establish if the parents have ever been shown as this indicates breed standard.

Meeting the breeding pair will also help you to get an idea of the size the kitten will reach and give an indication of personality as the mother in particular influences this.

Medical documentation

Finally, request proof from the breeder that the kitten has had its vaccinations, been dewormed and declared fit by a vet. The breeder must also provide you with a health guarantee. If he or she refuses, be very suspicious.

The kitten's temperament

This, as stated earlier, will be hinted at by the temperament and nature of the kitten's mother. However, the breeder will have – or should have – spent a lot of time with the kittens. Ask him or her about the temperament and personality of the kittens on offer or of the one that you are interested in.

Of course, your own observations while you watch the kittens play and when you interact will also tell you a lot about them. It is not hard to see which kittens are shy, extroverted, adventurous, playful and so on. You know what you are looking for in your Peterbald companion so watch for those qualities.

Chapter 6: Your new Peterbald kitten or cat

1) The first important few hours

You must never reach your newly arrived kitten or cat or try to cuddle him or her in the beginning. If your cat is not nervous by nature, it may just come to you on its own. What you should do, however, is visit the cat regularly. Walk into the bonding room, sit on the floor or a low chair for a while and call to him or her in a voice that is soothing. Even if it takes several sessions to get your cat to even greet you, don't lose your patience.

In case there are children in your family, make sure that they visit the cat only when they are accompanied by an adult, preferably you. This is very important in the initial days. The reason to take this precaution is that children often get excited at the sight of a kitten or cat. If they startle the new arrival, he or she might become anxious or frightened and scratch or bite the child. So, never let children near the cat without proper supervision.

2) Settling in

Bringing you new Peterbald home for the fist time is both exciting and a little scary. It should be the start of a wonderful long relationship so one must begin well. Keep in mind that there is a great deal that is new for the kitten or cat to adjust to; don't try and do it all at once.

If you work, try to collect your kitten or cat at a time, for example a Saturday morning, that will allow you to spend the whole weekend with him or her to make the transition easier and so you can bond. The time you take to bond with your new Peterbald is an important investment in your relationship that will stand you both in good stead for many years to come. You need to take the time and make an effort to get to know each other.

Chapter 6: Your new Peterbald kitten or cat

When you get to your home with your new Peterbald, it is recommended that you restrict him or her to just one or two rooms initially. Firstly, too much too soon can be overwhelming for a kitten or even an adult cat whose sense of hearing and smell is far more acute than ours. Secondly, housetraining is a little easier for you if your kitten is not allowed to go everywhere at the beginning. Finally, it allows you to bond with your cat and have control over how and when your Peterbald meets the other members of the household.

Don't be concerned or offended if the first thing your new kitten or cat's does when you get home is go into hiding. It might choose to crawl back into the carrier it arrived in or find another spot. It's not a bad idea to provide a few hiding spots that are easy to get into and out of. When your new Peterbald is ready it will emerge and begin to cautiously explore the new room it finds itself in. Don't force the issue; wait till he or she is ready to come out of hiding.

It can be a good idea to close the new arrival into a room and leave it on its own for an hour or so to give it a chance to calm down. Make sure that you have placed food and water in the room along with bedding and a cat litter box. Keep in mind that cats are clean creatures so don't place the litter box near the food and water bowls. Leaving a few toys in the room will also help your new companion begin to relax.

As I mentioned, cats have very acute hearing and smell. Your home is going to present your Peterbald with a host of sounds and smells that are new and sometimes intimidating. Things that are ordinary to us will sound very loud and scary to a newly arrived kitten or cat. To help him or her with this, there are a few guidelines to follow.

When you talk to your new kitten do so softly and don't pick it up too often. The sound and smell of you is new, too. Also, don't play music or the TV very loud. Wait to use the vacuum cleaner until your Peterbald has bonded with you and started to settle in.

At the very least, don't vacuum the room your kitten is placed in when it first arrives so that it has a non-threatening space. Hosting parties or dinner parties and having a line of people trooping in and out to admire or meet your new cat is also not a good idea.

3) Bringing home an adult Peterbald

An adult cat needs to be treated differently to a kitten. You need to take a few additional steps before bringing an adult Peterbald home.

First, an adult cat will usually take a little longer to settle than a kitten. Why? Because adult cats, like adult people, have a history and past experiences that result in established patterns of behaviour along with likes and dislikes. If you can find out what these are it will help you and your new Peterbald. If you get your cat from a breeder you can find about its past and interactions with people and other animals. If your new cat comes from a shelter you may not be able to get any information and will have to be guided by your cat's reactions.

You can also ask about food, toy and activity likes and dislikes. Being able to provide things you know your new companion is familiar with and enjoys will help him or her settle more easily. You could also enquire about things that the cat finds frightening. For instance, I once had a cat that was affectionate, laid-back, funny and usually fairly fearless. However, he was terrified of plastic bags! Somewhere in his past something unpleasant with a plastic bag had happened. I made a point never to have one anywhere near him.

Adult cats, if necessary, can be kept in a cat carrier for a few days. The carrier should be placed in the room that the cat will be confined to once it leaves the carrier. In fact, the carrier can be left in an out-of-the-way place permanently for use by your cat when it feels frightened, anxious or under the weather.

Just as with a kitten, there must always be food – preferably one the cat is familiar with and likes – and fresh water available. A litter box is also necessary.

When kittens and cats are accustomed to the sound and scent of their new owner it's important to spend as much time as possible with it as part of the settling in phase. Once there is less likelihood of accidents and your new Peterbald has left the room it was initially confined to, it's important to keep your kitten or cat company as it explores the entire home. Only when it has examined everything and every room will it decide which spots will be its resting, sleeping and hiding places.

Your new adult Peterbald needs to be watched. If your cat is not eating or using the litter box, showing signs of restlessness, being very vocal or scratching or licking excessively you may need to consult a vet as these are possible signs of stress and unhappiness.

4) *Preparing your family for a pet*

It is not only you and your home that must be ready for your new arrival. Everyone in the house must be prepared. Young children especially are usually so delighted to see a pet that they might shout, rush at or attempt to pick it up. This would not be what your Peterbald needs!

All the occupants of your home need to be informed about the cat that will be joining the household: when it will arrive, what it will look like, the changes that must be made both during the settling in phase and afterwards, to be patient and give the cat time and space to adjust and not to expect or try to handle or play with it immediately. With the Peterbald the waiting period before it is ready to have social and fun time with the family shouldn't be too long as they are so playful and gregarious by nature.

You will also need to make sure everybody knows about feeding, the litter box requirements, not feeding the cat unhealthy treats, keeping medicines and other poisons safely put away and keeping doors and windows closed until the initial period is safely negotiated.

Also, given cats love to explore and will sometimes go to sleep in odd places, the family must get into the habit of checking inside large appliances such as washing machines, tumble dryers and dishwashers before turning them on.

5) Make time for your new cat

One can't say this often enough: the Peterbald cat loves and needs attention! It's not necessary to play with it immediately because it is unlikely to feel like playing until it is feeling relaxed and settled, but you must spend time in the same room with it and speak to it in a friendly and soothing tone.

Just sit in the room and give your new companion time to get used to your scent and the way you sound, look and move. Family members can take turns spending time with the new arrival but at the beginning it should just be you.

Playtime

This can start in earnest with your new cat once it is used to the new surroundings. How can you tell your cat or kitten is ready? Your Peterbald will emerge from hiding and want to include you in his or her territory. You will know you have been accepted and marked when your new companion rubs its head, body or face on you to leave their scent or pheromones. You are now their person!

Even if your new cat now rubs itself against your legs it may still resist overtures from you. If you reach out to stroke or touch the cat or kitten and it backs off you can either leave it and give it a little more time or your could lure it with toys… A shoe lace or piece of string pulled along the ground is pretty irresistible to the majority of cats who will immediately give chase and pounce. A high energy and interactive game like this is the ideal ice breaker between you and your new Peterbald.

Chapter 6: Your new Peterbald kitten or cat

6) Complicated scenarios

You will have to do a little extra work if you are introducing your new Peterbald into a household in which there is a child, a dog or another cat. If you have children, dogs or cats there are already hierarchies and pecking orders in place that your new arrival will have to fit into. However, there are steps one can take that will make the transition much smoother for all concerned.

Introducing your Peterbald to your dog

Another of the many advantages of this breed is that they get on well with dogs. That is assuming of course that the dog is cat-friendly. No breed will be comfortable with a dog that thinks cats are for chasing or make great snacks! If you are not quite sure how your dog will behave there are a few steps you can take to make sure that there are not problems.

While your new Peterbald is in the bonding room for the post-arrival period don't let the dog in. What does help is to get them used to each other's scents before they meet in person. An easy way to achieve this is by feeding them on either side of the door. Of course if your dog starts barking or scratching at the door you must move him or her further away and then move the bowl closer gradually. Eventually they will become familiar with each other's smell. It's time to move on to the next step once they can both quietly get on with their meals with just the door between them.

When the first face-to-face introduction takes place, it is wise to put a leash on both the dog and the Peterbald. In all probability your cat will be interested and fairly relaxed. Once you are sure that your dog is not going to give chase and isn't showing any signs of aggression, take the leash off the cat. It will help considerably if your dog is trained with basic commands such as, "Sit" and "Stay". If it isn't, consider doing so. You can also use treats to reward your dog each time it interacts positively with your cat.

Even though the Peterbald does interact well with dogs and many times will play with and even sleep curled up with a dog, keep in mind that dogs and cats can be unpredictable. Until you are 100% that there is harmony between then, especially if your Peterbald is still a kitten, don't leave them alone together. Even a playful bite from a dog could badly injure or even kill a kitten.

If your dog is just not accepting your new cat and continues to bark and or snap at it you may have to get professional advice about how you can modify behaviour and get your dog to calm down. Alternatively, you may have to return the cat…

Introducing your Peterbald to an existing cat or cats

If there is already a resident cat in your home, expect your new Peterbald to become more dominant with familiarity. It is stressful to your old pet to deal with the fact that there is another cat in the house. Quite obviously, it is stressful for you as well to make sure that your older cat does not feel neglected or out of place. You need to follow a process to make the situation more relaxed for you, your older cat and your new Peterbald.

The first direct interaction should preferably be scheduled over a weekend so that you have all day to spend with the new cat and your cat-in-residence. This way, you can make sure that there are no unpleasant incidents and so that you can intervene if needs be.

It is usually best to get your older cat and new Peterbald to interact during a meal time. Some growling and hissing, especially initially, is to be expected as both will want to assert themselves to some degree. However, it will not be entirely aggressive. To make sure that it does not get out of hand, though, you must place their feeding bowls at opposite ends of the room and you must stay with them. Once the feeding is done, separate them again.

Most cats are territorial by nature although your Peterbald's main territory will be you. Make sure you establish the boundaries for both the cats. When your new cat is out of the confinement from its bonding or settling in room, you might want to make a special corner for him that is not too close to the existing space of you resident cat. Just place the feeding bowl and the cat bed in the designated area with your cat's favourite toys.

The interactions between your cats must be gradual so they become used to each other and neither feels threatened or rushed. You can try the blanket switching technique with cats so that they become more used to each other's scents or pheromones. When they are accustomed to each others' scent, they will become comfortable with each other. Increase the time they spend with each other slowly. Only leave them together unsupervised when you are sure that they are relaxed in each other's company. Until then you must never leave them unattended in the same space. This is especially true for night times when cats are most active.

If you have more than one cat at home, you will notice that one of the resident cats will take the initiative to introduce the new cat to the existing group. If this happens you are in luck as they will probably handle the situation far better than you could!

It is not uncommon for cats to not get along immediately although the Peterbald gets on with other cats far better than most other breeds. But, if your resident cat and the new kitten or cat doesn't hit it off make sure you don't punish either of them. You just need to separate them when they get anxious. You must understand that this behaviour is purely instinctive. With regular interactions, the cats will learn to live together peacefully and will decide who is who in terms of seniority or pecking order.

Your new Peterbald and babies or toddlers

As a rule, Peterbald cats are tolerant of children and gentle with them. However, it is quite possible – and perfectly natural – that young children will get excited. This excitement usually manifests itself as excited shouts or squeals when they first catch sight of the new kitty.

In addition to these noises which will be very loud and alarming for a new cat, a child also looks, behaves and smells very different from an adult. This unfamiliarity is not only distressing for the cat but also potentially dangerous for a child. There are some rules to introduce your child to the new cat that will reduce the trauma and possibility of injuries to either the cat or the child.

Make sure that your new cat and your child or children have regular interactions as soon as your new Peterbald has started to settle and is comfortable around you. At no point should you allow the child to venture alone into the room where the new cat is still settling. You can teach your child to call the cat soothingly and even just watch the cat quietly until it gets accustomed to the child or children's presence.

It's also important to teach children not to run at or grab at a cat as that will alarm it greatly as it won't understand this is a gesture of enthusiasm and affection! Children also need to be told that the cat is not a toy. You must constantly remind your child to be gentle. He or she must know that pulling the ear or tail of the cat can be really painful for it. Also, a cat that is hurt or angry may also instinctively retaliate and cause a child some pain from a scratch or a nip. If this happens, comfort your child but don't punish the cat.

Scent is very important in the animal world. In fact, many animals relate to things purely on the basis of their smell. Cats use other senses too but scent shouldn't be underestimated. It is therefore a good idea to let your child handle some of the cat's items such as bedding or toys so that their scent is left behind for the cat to get used to. If he or she is old enough you can give your child a responsibility such as filling up the food or water bowl.

With much younger children like toddlers it is not realistic to give them responsibility for caring for the cat, but you could use the sock technique to introduce them to each other. Rub one of your toddler's socks on the cat's cheek. Then, let the toddler wear the sock. Because of this rubbing off of the scent, the cat will smell its own pheromones on the sock and view the toddler as a friend that it can trust.

Peterbald cat owners all stress how tolerant and flexible their cats are. They are very gentle and loving cats and will therefore usually make truly great companions for children to play with. Most children and Peterbald cats develop close bonds.

Over and above the time you must spend getting your cat settled, introduced to the other residents, cuddling and playing with your new kitten or cat you need to start training… for both your sakes!

7) *Training*

While the Peterbald is an extremely intelligent cat it is still a cat. This means that your kitten will be as good at training you as you are at training it. The ease with which you train a cat increases in direct proportion to the degree to which they want to be trained. In your favour, in addition to their intelligence, is the Peterbald cat's desire to please.

Scratch Training

Getting a cat to use a scratching post rather than your furniture is usually fairly easy. Cats naturally look for a rough surface to sharpen their claws. Incorporate the scratching post into play sessions in the first few days. Scratch the surface of the post with your finger nail or nails. The sound alone will get your kitten interested. As soon as he or she tries to catch your finger they will be introduced to a surface they like the feel of. Continue to do this for a few days and your smart Peterbald should stick to the post and leave your sofa and table legs alone.

You can add to the appeal of a scratching post by spraying it with catnip. Few cats can resist the smell. Remember, though, to reapply the spray every few days as it does wear off or fade over time.

In addition, I had a cat that decided the edges of my sofas were the best surface for nail sharpening. Clapping my hands and trying to reason with him did not work. So, I used broad packaging tape along the sections he was energetically targeting. The first time he tried it again he didn't enjoy either the feel or smell of the tape. After only 2 days I could remove the tape and he never touched the sofas again.

Litter-Box Training

This is an important area of training as nobody wants a cat that is not housetrained. In this regard you will be assisted by both the intelligence of the Peterbald and the inherently fastidious and clean feline nature.

Keep in mind that a kitten is a baby. Like human babies it will be busy playing or doing something and not realize till the last minute that it needs to urinate or defecate. For this reason you need to expect the odd accident and be sensible about where you place the litter box. Your kitten will sometimes need to get to it in a hurry.

The best places to put a litter box are away from areas where the cat eats, where food is stored or prepared and in a quite place (cats like privacy too). A corner is also usually ideal. If your house is large or has more than one level, it can be a good idea to have more than one litter box. Also, if you have more than one cat, you may well need a litter box per cat. Finally, don't move the litter box around so you cat or kitten knows where to find it.

It is very important to show your kitten where the litter box is. One needs to establish a routine:

- ✓ Place your kitten gently into the litter box a few minutes after a meal and after he or she wakes up
- ✓ Be patient. Give your kitten time to walk around and sniff the litter box
- ✓ The instinct to dig and bury waste usually emerges on its own. If it doesn't, gently take one of the kitten's front paws and show him or her how to dig and scratch in the sand. Alternatively, dig a little hole in the (clean) litter with your fingers while the kitten watches. He or she will probably join in and then carry on digging on its own
- ✓ Every time your Peterbald kitten uses the litter box give it lots of praise and cuddles
- ✓ Don't ever shout at or otherwise frighten a kitten in a litter box because he or she will make a negative association.

Furthermore, if you are spending time with your kitten and watching it you will notice the signs that it needs to use the box. Don't rush at or alarm it; gently pick it up and place it in the litter tray.

Once the litter box has been used the likelihood that the kitten will return increases as his or her scent has been left there. In the event of an accident – and these will happen – you can take some of the waste and place it in the box as this might help to increase the scent levels.

Don't shout at or hit a kitten that has had an accident. It won't know what you are angry about and will begin to fear you or feel nervous. It is far better if you praise good behaviour – the use of the litter box – and intervene when you see an accident is imminent in order to re-enforce the connection.

In order to encourage your kitten to make the transition from litter box to outdoor area or garden, you just need to slowly move the litter box closer and closer to the external door that the kitten, and later the cat, will use. Eventually you will move the litter box to just outside the door. When you see your kitten or cat in the litter box and about to use it, pick it up and show it a suitable patch of earth that is soft enough to dig in. In time he or she will pick their favourite spots.

Toilet Training

Most of us are happy to teach our kittens and cats to use a litter box and then, if we can, gradually move into the garden. There are, however, some patient cat owners who want their cat to use the toilet. The nature and temperament of the Peterbald certainly will help with this more complex training, especially if you disguise it as a game.

The first step is to place the litter box on the floor, right next to the toilet, for a few days. Thereafter you will need to gradually raise the litter box until it is at the same height as the toilet seat. At the same time as raising the box, gradually decrease the amount of litter in it.

The next stage in the process involves moving the box onto the seat in 1" (2.5cm) increments. Eventually the box will be directly over the seat and there should only be a very thin layer of litter left.

At this point the litter box should be replaced with a training box. You have two options: a commercially available product or a homemade one. If you opt for the latter you can fasten wax paper, plastic or foil over the toilet bowl, under the seat. Sprinkle a handful of litter onto the training box. A word of caution: make sure whatever material you use is strong enough to hold the weight of the kitten or cat when it steps onto it or jumps up. If he or she falls in the toilet that's it; you can forget toilet training!

The next stage is to cut a hole that is 1" (2.5cm) in diameter in the material you have used. Gradually increase the diameter until the material is almost cut right back to the bowl. By now the sprinkling of litter should be gone entirely.

Finally, remove the training box or seat. Don't teach your Peterbald to flush the toilet; they can enjoy it so much it will drive you nuts and waste a lot of water!

Lying on his or her back

This training will make your life much easier and your Peterbald more relaxed. Given you are going to have cut nails, wash and clean and do the odd examination, getting your cat accustomed to lying on its back is important and helpful. It will be so much easier to, for example, cut nails if you have a relaxed cat lying on its back rather than a kitty that is struggling and thrashing about, stressing you both and running the risk of nicks and cuts.

Lying on their back is not a natural position for cats; it's a sign of submission and leaves them very vulnerable. But if you get your kitten used to it early on by making it part of a game it should be fine. As you play with it, roll the kitten gently onto its back, love and stroke its little fat tummy and tell your Peterbald how clever and gorgeous it is.

Of course a treat also won't go amiss. After a while your kitten may roll onto its back during play and then get used to being held and carried that way. I have a cat that will only be held if she is on her back.

Water and bathing

As with lying on their backs, this is also important training in order to reduce stress levels in your Peterbald and you because a weekly bath and often daily washes will be a feature of your lives. If you get a kitten from a breeder then he or she may already have bathed the kitten and made it more accustomed to water. If that is the case consider yourself lucky and maintain regular baths.

We all know that, usually, cats dislike – even hate – water. It is unlikely that your Peterbald will ever enjoy having a bath although now and then one does. The best you can hope for is that your kitten and cat will tolerate the process and not become distressed or aggressive.

Be as gentle and as relaxed about it as possible. Your Peterbald will pick up if you are anxious or stressed. Make bath time as fun as you can. Make washing feel more like being cuddled than lathered. Talk to your cat during bath time and reward him or her with a special treat afterwards.

Swimming pools

Once your cat is used to water introduce it to the swimming pool. It is vital that you show your cat where to get out of the water and give it enough practice in doing so that your Peterbald will be able to get itself out of the water even if you are not there to help.

Doing tricks

Some feel that cats shouldn't be trained to do tricks because it is somehow beneath their dignity. This is a very personal choice. Actually it will probably be your cat's decision rather than yours.

There is no doubt that the intelligence and eagerness to entertain and please found in the Peterbald means that one can train them to do tricks more easily than many breeds. Remember, though, that their intelligence might just mean that they get you to do tricks…

There are numerous instances of cats that play fetch. As with any behaviour you want to reinforce and encourage, rewards are very important as motivators for your cat. With a Peterbald the treat doesn't have to be edible because your cat will be addicted to affection and cuddles. So, stroking him or her or playing a fun game will also be an effective reward.

Some cats also sit on command. This can be achieved by holding a treat above the cat's head and saying, "Sit!" If he or she does, hand over the treat. If not, repeat the command while gently but firmly pushing the cat's bottom down and then giving a treat. Keep this routine up until the cat sits when asked to.

Agility training

Agility training is something you can do with your Peterbald just because it is fun for both of you rather than because you want to enter or compete in agility shows or contests. Of course you can choose to compete in these increasingly popular competitions. Agility training is a wonderful way to exercise and stimulate an indoor cat.

Your Peterbald will be ideal for agility activities for several reasons. Firstly, these are intelligent cats that thrive on new activities and challenges. Secondly, they are easy to train thanks to both their intelligence and enthusiasm. Finally, your cat will love playing and spending this one-on-one time with you.

You don't need special equipment for agility training. You can use things around the house to set up an agility course that provides things to jump over and tunnels to run through. A paper bag cut open at both ends makes good a tunnel. A wooden, long handled utensil such as a spoon balanced on top of two mugs or rolls of toilet paper will make a perfectly good hurdle. Of course you can buy equipment from a supplier. Either way, remember that you must build an agility course that should be like a playground for your cat. Keep your cat's age and size in mind so you don't expect too much or push too hard. It must be fun for both of you.

You can start agility training when a kitten is really young. Just be patient and gentle and stop when your kitty shows signs of being tired or losing interest. Remember this is supposed to be fun, not military boot camp! Don't ever force your cat to do anything. If your cat seems tired or indicates it has had enough give it a rest and try again later or the next day. It is important, though, to do these agility activities with your cat every day.

Using a toy of some kind that will grab your kitten or cat's attention and lure it through a tunnel or hoop or over an obstacle is a very effective training tool. There are cat toys with feathers on them that are not too expensive and are ideal for this purpose. Wiggle the toy at the end of the tunnel or other side of an obstacle to entice your cat through or over it. A cat's natural desire to chase and pounce will work with you. As with any training, treats should be used to reward the cat each time it does something correctly or well. You can also use a clicker bought from a vet store. Clicker training means that when your cat gets it right you 'click' and give it a treat. Do not forget the treat must be accompanied by verbal praise and cuddles.

8) How long a Peterbald can be left alone

If you asked your Peterbald this question the answer would be along the lines of, "Not at all… Please!" These affectionate and gregarious cats do not like being alone. If you need to go out for a few hours your cat will cope, but he or she won't be happy. If you will be away at work each day, all day, then you must get your cat a companion so that he or she does not become stressed, lonely and even depressed. You don't have to have a second Peterbald; just so long as it is a friendly animal and the two of them get along well.

9) Transporting your Peterbald

Much of this is really common sense… Never drive or travel in a car with a cat sitting on your lap or on the seat. The cat could very easily become frightened, jump onto the driver or get under the pedals and cause an accident. Use a carry cage or a cat basket to contain the cat. Don't use a cardboard box as the cat may escape or claw its way out if very frightened.

If you must leave your cat in the car on a warm day, make sure that the car is parked in a cool spot and that the windows are down slightly to allow some airflow.

Before leaving on a long journey, restrict the cat's food and water intake for 2 to 3 hours. In hot weather the cat will need to have a drink now and then throughout the day.

10) Keeping your Peterbald warm

Because of their hairless or near hairless condition your cat is in effect naked. This means that he or she will feel the cold far more than you will in your clothes. Your Peterbald must be kept warm including when you are not there. Your heating bill is going to go up if you live in a cold climate and need to run central heating or other heating systems. Alternatively, you could purchase a heated cat bed or a heating pad. There are various models that are available. Remember, though, that these cats burn easily so keep an eye on the temperature. Your Peterbald might enjoy wearing a garment of some sort but many cats don't enjoy the sensation at all and do all they can to get out of the alien and restricting object. There is also a chance that clothing could irritate your cat's skin or even set up an infection.

11) To microchip your cat or not

The reason to micro-chip is to help to trace it if it is lost. A microchip is one aspect of cat identification. The other is a break-away collar with a disc. Although a chip can be effective, it is not fool-proof. The down side is that having a chip will only help if someone takes your cat to a shelter if it gets lost. Also, while most animal shelters have scanners and use them, this is not true of all of them. This is why also having a break-away collar and tag is a good idea in addition to a microchip.

The procedure is fairly simple and should, preferably, be done by a vet. A large needle is used to place the chip, which is about the size of a grain of rice, under the skin between the cat's shoulder blades. A special scanner can read the unique number on the chip. The procedure to insert the chip only takes a few seconds and the sensation is the same as having blood drawn. In other words, there is a little pain and discomfort but it is very brief.

There is an extremely small possibility of complications after the chip implant. For instance, a few animals have developed tumours at the site where the chip was placed. This is, however, statistically very unlikely.

The cost of micro-chipping at time of writing is in the region of $50 in America and up to £40 in the UK depending on when it's done and who does it. If you are going to have this procedure done, you can take your cat in to the vet from the age of 12 weeks onwards.

The chips used in different parts of the world also utilize different frequencies. The UK and Europe use a 134.2 kilohertz chip while a 125 and 128 kilohertz chip is used in America. If you are going to take your cat across a border you should check on the requirements as some countries have regulations about both chip date and type.

Chapter 7: Feeding your Peterbald

1) What to feed your kitten and how often

A kitten's nutritional needs and digestive capabilities are not the same as those of an adult cat. For the first year of your cat's life you will need to give it a balanced diet using a good quality kitten food that you can purchase either from your vet or a pet shop. If you are unsure what brand to buy, ask your vet for advice.

If you decide you want to feed your little Peterbald raw meat you must keep in mind that this diet won't provide all the nutrition and trace elements that a growing cat needs. As a result you will also need to give your kitty a nutritional supplement. The bottom line is that the nutrition a kitten gets will lay the foundations for future health!

2) What to feed adult cats and how often

The Peterbald has a higher metabolism than other cats; it helps them to stay warm. As a result, they eat a great deal. Giving your cat small portions regularly helps to control body heat and weight and protects their sensitive digestive systems.

Standard foods and diet

Eating canned cat food every day is not recommended. Many cat owners feel that canned food once or twice a week is more than adequate. Also keep in mind that some canned foods are better than others. It's important to read the label on the tin to ensure that the contents do not contain sugar or inferior meats. You should specifically look for canned foods that list meat or chicken as the first or second ingredient. Your cat's food should be served at room temperature and the Peterbald diet requires the right balance of protein and fat.

Just like people, cats like variety in their diet. If you decide to change your cat's diet you need to do so gradually. Keep an eye on your cat and if there is any evidence of gastric problems you need to reconsider the food your Peterbald is being given.

Dry food is a healthy option for your cat. Not only does it provide nutrition it may also help to keep your cat's teeth clean and its gums healthy if you get a correctly formulated food. Investing in a food dispenser is a good idea as it means that your cat can snack even when you are not around, day or night.

Just keep in mind that a cat that is eating more dry food will require a lot of water. There must always be a good supply of fresh clean water available for you kitten or cat!

Peterbald cats love food and are keen to try anything. A word of warning, though: do not, I repeat not, give your cat human's food! This applies to scraps when you are cooking, treats from your plate during meals or leftovers. Firstly, your cat may be exposed to food stuffs that are toxic for him or her. Secondly, your cat will put on weight. Furthermore, you will end up with a cat that begs or even steals food.

Some Peterbald owners believe very strongly in a diet that consists only of raw food and bones. Proponents of this diet state that their cats are healthier overall. Others think that any balanced, varied diet will be healthy. Yet other cat lovers believe that foods containing grains should be avoided.

Preventative nutrition

Let's talk now about "preventative nutrition" which is the best kind of nutrition for your cat. If you think that your cat is "fine" and continue to give it foods that are not really recommended, there is a chance that it will at some stage develop serious health issues. For instance, cats that are constantly and exclusively given dry foods can suddenly develop the following conditions:

- Inflammatory Bowel Disease
- Asthma due to allergens
- Inflamed bladder leading to painful elimination
- Blocked urinary tract that, if severe, can led to rupture of the bladder and death
- Feline Diabetes
- Kidney stones.

These conditions can be prevented with a little attention to the food that your kitten and later your cat is given. As a pet owner, it is your responsibility to choose a diet that ensures longevity and long term health benefits for your Peterbald. In order to understand preventive nutrition, here are some things that you need to know about the nutritional requirements of cats.

Firstly, carbohydrates are very damaging to a cat's health. They cause diabetes which is currently one of the most common diseases in domesticated cats. Cats are carnivores by design and nature, so feeding them carbohydrates or plant based proteins will upset their digestive systems and potentially lead to more serious conditions or problems.

Secondly, the thirst drive is low in cats. It is therefore necessary for them to drink water along with their food. In the wild, the food that cats eat consists of almost 75% of water. Domestic cats will never make up for the lack of water by lapping from their water bowls. Water is extremely important to keep the urinary tract system healthy. If the cat's body does not receive the necessary amount of water, there may be harmful repercussions such as urinary tract obstructions and / or infections. These problems are not common in cats that normally consume canned foods or other forms of wet food.

In addition, there are no benefits to the dental health of your cat from dry foods unless they are specialised foods. There are some that have been specially developed by manufacturers for cats and their dental needs. These special – and sometimes expensive – foods are available from a vet or good pet store.

However, there are some experts who claim that these foods don't actually work either because, although several dry food companies may claim this, there is no clear scientific basis to prove that this is true for cats. If you are unsure, approach a cat association or a third party whose only concern is cat's welfare.

In short, preventive nutrition is the only way to ensure that your Peterbald enjoys long lasting benefits from the food that it eats. Not all pet owners understand the principle that preventive nutrition is based upon. The five principles of preventive nutrition that you can follow to ensure optimized and holistic nutrition for your cat are:

- ✓ There must always be fresh water available
- ✓ Your cat needs to snack a great deal to maintain body temperature so food must always be available
- ✓ Provide a mixture of dry and wet or canned food
- ✓ Avoid foods that contain grains and corbohydrates
- ✓ Provide a balanced diet that is not too high in proteins or fats.

Food formulated by experts

Creating the right food for cats is not easy. There is a certain amount of expertise that is very important to ensure that all the key ingredients and nutrients are present in the formulae. There are specialized pet nutritionists who work to provide your cat with an optimized formula to ensure the correct nutrition. These foods are tested and tried for their effects before they are released for pet owners to use for their cats. There are several feeding trials that are conducted to understand how effective the formula is in enhancing the health of your cat.

According to association officials in America, feeding trials are the most important tools to understand the quality of a pet food. Those that have undergone feeding trials are given to the pets under recommended guidelines which must be strictly followed to make sure that the cats get the right nutrition from them.

The quality controls involved in the development and testing of these foods begins with the concern with safety. There are several manufacturers that produce these foods in their own facilities and they are, generally, thought to be more trustworthy for a few reasons.

Firstly, the quality control is better as the source of the ingredients and all the associated processes are monitored effectively. All the foods that are manufactured on site are held until they meet all the safety guidelines recommended for the product. As a result, issues like Salmonella contamination are effectively prevented.

In addition, when you purchase a certain cat food, check if the food has been 'manufactured by' or just has been 'distributed by' the brand that you have chosen. If the brand that you are purchasing is also the manufacturing unit, it is easier to register complaints with respect to the quality of the food provided as you can report any concerns that you have on the quality of the food to the manufacturer directly.

There are several brands and types of cat foods available and they are formulated for cats of various activity levels, ages and breeds. Some also help to prevent certain problems such as hairball formation (not a problem your Peterbald will suffer from of course).

There are several "life stage foods" that have been formulated because the nutritional requirements vary from kittens to adult and senior cats. However, there is another variety called the "ALL life stage" food that is available in some countries. This is definitely not widely recommended as it may lead to malnutrition or even excessive nutrition which could lead to several serious health issues in your cat.

If you find it hard to make a decision with regards to the right food for your feline friend, ask for help or advice from your vet or pet store salesperson. He or she should be able to help based on the breed and age of your cat.

3) What not to feed your Peterbald cat

Usually cat owners think that their pets instinctively know what is best for them. Cats are known to be picky eaters but there is little evidence that suggests that a cat knows what is right for it and what is wrong. Perhaps in the wild cats follow their instincts and get the right nutrition. However, with domesticated cats the varieties of foods that are available will make them interested in all the wrong sorts of things.

There are a number of food stuffs that should not be given to your Peterbald or any cat for that matter:

- Onions, chives and garlic: at best your kitty's digestive system will be unhappy. At worst, eating onion regularly or a large amount can lead to anaemia.
- Milk and other dairy products: despite the clichés such as, "You look like the cat that ate the cream" and images of cats lapping milk, most cats are lactose intolerant.
- Caffeine: this can be fatal for cats. There is caffeine in tea, cocoa, carbonated drinks, many energy drinks and some cough and cold remedies. It is not only found in coffee.
- Chocolate: it contains theobromine which is highly toxic for cats and can lead to death. The darker the chocolate the more poisonous it is for cats.
- Liver: kittens especially shouldn't be fed liver as it is high in vitamin A. Too much of the vitamin can lead to severe bone problems and malformations.
- Raisins and grapes: for reasons that are still unclear, these can lead to kidney failure.
- Sweets/candy, diet foods and drinks, baked goods and some toothpaste: some of these contain the sugar substitute Xylitol which can cause liver failure in cats.
- Raw eggs: avidin, the protein in the egg white, inhibits the absorption of biotin, a vitamin necessary for skin health.
- Alcohol (yes, some – who don't deserve a pet – think it's funny to get a pet drunk): it has the same effect on a cat's

brain and liver as it does on ours. The difference is that 3 teaspoons of whiskey will kill a 5lb or 2.3kg cat.
- Yeast dough: uncooked dough is never recommended for a cat. If your cat eats dough there is a chance that it will actually begin to rise inside the cat's stomach. During this expansion, the dough may stretch the stomach and abdomen causing pain or internal injury. In addition, the cat may suffer alcohol poisoning as the yeast ferments.
- Dog food: A bite once in a while will not harm your cat too much. However, the formula used in dog food is obviously for dogs and therefore definitely not suitable for cats. Cat food is packed with the proteins and vitamins necessary to fulfil a cat's nutritional requirements. On the other hand, dog foods may contain plant proteins that are not suitable for cats. If your Peterbald regularly consumes dog food, it might become malnourished.

Often being cautious isn't enough and your cat might make its way into your kitchen or pantry and have a generous helping of restricted or forbidden foods. There is no need to be unduly alarmed. Find out what it is that your cat has eaten and, in most cases, your vet will be able to provide an antidote or treatment to take care of the situation for you.

The golden rule is to stick to food and treats formulated for cats. No matter how much you think of your Peterbald as a person, he or she is a cat. And be careful about what you leave within easy reach of your cat.

4) Treats

Treats are both a way of saying you love your cat and of rewarding good or desirable behaviour. While a game with you or a cuddle from you is probably what your Peterbald likes the most, treats can be useful.

Using treats as part of an exercise routine can work, especially if you live in a smaller home or your cat is purely an indoor cat.

You could hide a couple of dry treats around the house each day and your cat will get some exercise dashing about finding them. It is a good idea to start this routine when your Peterbald is still young.

If you are unsure what treats are healthy for your cat, purchase them directly from your vet or you could ask the staff there for recommendations or suggestions. An alternative is to make your own treats by cooking up a little meat or chicken and giving your cat a small piece at a time.

Treats also don't have to be in edible form. What about a fun toy or some catnip?

Chapter 8: Grooming your Peterbald

Peterbald cats require thorough and regular grooming. The lack of any hair or a thick coat means that you need to deal with the oils that build up on the skin and the wax, oil and so on in the ears. Hairless male cats need a daily wipe-down of the tail area in order to prevent the build-up of excess oil that might cause blackheads at the base of the tail.

As with other cats, nails need trimming and teeth must be cleaned. A big advantage is that the Peterbald enjoys water and bath time!

1) Bathing your Peterbald

There is no getting around this: you must give your cat a bath regularly in order to keep it healthy… and your furniture and clothes free of oil marks if your Peterbald is hairless. Hairless cats will probably need a weekly bath. Peterbalds with a flock, velour or brush coat need a monthly bath. Don't bath you cat too often, though, or the skin becomes too dry.

I suggest that you get a number of things before you fetch your kitten or cat. You need to run warm, *not* hot, water into the bathtub, basin, sink or container. The water must be body temperature or your cat could develop dandruff.

As the water runs, add a small amount of shampoo to the water. Also, put a clean towel close by. Truly adoring cat owners will warm the towel slightly too! Putting your cat into a bath or shower with you is not recommended.

Place your Peterbald gently into the water and wet him or her using a cup, small jug or some other suitable receptacle. Once your cat is wet it's time for the shampoo. Some cats require more than one application; it depends on how oily the skin becomes. As with any animal, try not to get shampoo in your cat's eyes or water in its ears. Don't forget to wash the cat's bottom, feet and toes too.

Once you have rinsed off all the shampoo with clean water lift him or her out and wrap your cat in a towel. Talk soothingly to your cat throughout the bath. Ending the exercise with a treat of some kind in addition to praise and affection is a good idea!

2) Eye and face care

Cleaning your Peterbald cat's face and eyes can either be done in the bath or afterwards. Use soft wipes that won't lose any fluff or threads and wipe his or her face and around the eyes very gently so you remove dirt and excess oils.

The Peterbald's skin is sensitive, but you need to clean all the oil that has collected between the wrinkles in the face and neck or an infection may begin. Don't use soap or baby wipes around the eyes as this will irritate and inflame the eye.

3) Nail care and clipping

Nails should be trimmed or cut once or even twice a month. The warm water and shampoo will help to soften your cat's nails so do this part of grooming soon after bath time. You need to clean the nails and also the fold of skin above the nail where oil and dirt collects. Using an ear bud or Q-tip dipped in warm water usually does the trick. In order to trim the nails, use a small pair of fingernail clippers. Cut the nails with great care so as not to nick the skin or flesh around the nails. If your Peterbald is a wriggler and objects to the process you must enlist someone's help so that injuries are avoided.

4) Ear care

The hairless ear of the Peterbald can't filter dirt and dust particles the way other cat's ears can. This means that one of your jobs is to keep your kitten or cat's ears clean and free of wax and oil.

Chapter 8: Grooming your Peterbald

Use a cat-safe, gentle cleaning solution and good quality ear buds or Q-tips so that you don't deposit fibres and threads as you remove dirt. The Peterbald has large ears so you need to be systematic. A fairly good guide is to start at the outside and work in. Warning: don't put the Q-tip or ear bud too deep into the ear as you will damage it and cause a great deal of pain.

5) *Tooth care*

Dental care is very important and discussed in detail in chapter 9.

6) *Products to use*

As with cat litter and food, there is a wide choice when it comes to bath, cleaning or hygiene products for cats. If you are unsure about what would be best, be guided by a reputable breeder or by your vet when it comes to the best shampoo, moisturizer for hairless cats and ear cleaning solution.

The other items you will use are ear buds or Q-tips, cotton wipes or swabs, mild baby wipes and fingernail clippers. Just be sure to buy good quality and hypoallergenic or non-allergenic items.

Chapter 9: Your Peterbald's health

1) Finding a good vet

It is very important for you to have a reliable vet who you can trust with your pet. It is never a good idea to constantly change the vet who treats your Peterbald. Cats, as you know, do not appreciate change and most animals are reluctant to co-operate with vets. So, you must give your cat time to get accustomed to the scent, touch and voice of one vet. Once your cat is comfortable with him or her, it will be more relaxed during visits to the vet.

A vet is an important part of your cat's life and you must make sure you look for the perfect one to take care of your pet. There will be several large and small veterinary clinics around your town or city area. As a result, there may be a huge choice which can be confusing more than helpful when you set out to choose a vet for your Peterbald. The best way to look for a vet is to ask for recommendations from the breeder and your cat-owning friends and neighbours.

You must make an effort to look for someone who specializes in cat care. Alternatively, you can go to a vet practice that does at least have one or two vets who work mainly with cats. There are a few aspects that you might want to consider before you decide on a vet:

- o How far is the vet from your home?
- o Is the commuting time too long in event of an emergency?
- o Do you like the staff and find them confidence inspiring?

It is always better to find someone close to your house. It should preferably not take more than 15 minutes to drive down to your vet. Even if it is not an emergency, remember that your cat will not be particularly fond of long drives. Once you have found someone who seems to fit all the requirements, you can make a trial visit. The chemistry between your cat and the vet is extremely important if you want to make it a long-lasting relationship.

There are some things that will indicate how comfortable you and your pet will be in a particular clinic. Make the following observations if you are visiting for the first time.

- The waiting room must be clean and well maintained
- The ambience must be comforting for the cat so that it feels secure when it is being examined
- If it is a clinic shared by dogs and cats, how are they housed when they are admitted for hospital care?
- The people at the reception must be friendly. These people are going to be your point of contact in the coming sessions and you must be comfortable with them and trust them.

Once you are in the examination room, check how the vet interacts with both the pets and their owners. His or her tone must be soothing. The vet should be able to provide undivided attention to the animal being examined. He or she must also value your opinions about your cat's health and must be respectful towards you and your feelings. A vet should also be prepared to answer any questions you may have about the care, condition or treatment of your cat.

The personality of your vet plays an important part in the way he or she interacts with the animals being examined and treated. A vet must be genuinely passionate about his or her job. Without passion, you cannot be sure that a vet will go to all lengths to ensure the best for your Peterbald.

The vet you select must be good with cats and have a complete and up to date knowledge of the different practices and techniques that have evolved in veterinary practice. A vet must also make a conscious effort to upgrade his or her skills and knowledge.

Chapter 9: Your Peterbald's health

Once you are reassured about the behaviour of the vet towards you and your cat, you need to get down to the technical and legal aspects of this decision.

- ✓ Is the facility equipped to handle emergencies?
- ✓ How many cages or rooms do they have for the pets that have been admitted?
- ✓ Is every staff member appropriately educated or trained?
- ✓ Is the facility licensed?
- ✓ What are the costs for tests and surgeries?
- ✓ Is the pricing competitive enough?
- ✓ What, if any, pet insurance policies do they accept?
- ✓ Are emergencies handled after regular working hours?
- ✓ Who takes care of the pets when they are hospitalized?
- ✓ Are they open to alternative medicines and treatments?

Once you've received satisfactory answers to all these questions, you can be assured that this facility is best suited to your cat. Remember, the person you choose as your vet is going to be your partner in the wellbeing of your Peterbald for many years to come.

2) Preparing your Cat for a vet visit

Taking a cat to the vet is not easy... for either of you! Cats experience a lot of stress when they are travelling. As a result, it is best that you prepare your cat well for a visit to the vet. Here are five tips that will make the visit less stressful for your cat:

The pre vet visit routine

Cats require a good amount of mental preparation before they are taken to the vet.

Start by giving your Peterbald a thorough check up from head to toe at home. Look in its ears and mouth, run your hands over its limbs and feel its tummy. This is a more relaxed imitation of the examination that will take place in the vet's clinic. The idea is to get the cat used to being handled by the vet. Obviously in the event of an emergency this kind of preparation can't happen as there is no time.

Getting your cat used to the carrier is another way to make the visit less stressful. If your cat learns to associate the carrier with vet visits only, it might start to resist and fight being put into the carrier. On the other hand, if you create associations like play time or even fun outdoor visits with the carrier, your Peterbald might look forward to the positive activities and be less stressed. You can also designate the carrier as a nap place. Throw his or her favourite toys and treats inside the carrier to tempt your cat to go into the carrier and spend time in it.

Of course, the actual travel to the vet is going to create a great deal of stress in your cat. You can reduce this by being affectionate to him or her during the drive. Talk soothingly to him or her and, if possible, place the carrier in such a way that your Peterbald can see you. This should reduce his or her anxiety levels.

Make your car cat friendly

Most cats dislike cars and some are very frightened by the noise and the smell. Much of the resistance to the visit to the vet is not the clinic itself but is more connected to the journey to the vet. As previously mentioned, cats are usually only taken out in the car for their visit to the vet. As a result, they automatically associate cars with the negative experiences that they have had at the vet including injections, pain, illness and bad tasting medicines. It's therefore hardly surprising that few cats stay calm and relaxed inside a car.

However, you can help your cat make positive associations by including drives in the car in your daily routine. You can take the car for short distances too. Take the car to the park, for instance. You can even stop by at the vet's clinic for 5 minutes to get your cat used to the staff there.

The basic idea is to get your cat used to the car. He or she must learn to be calm and relaxed during these visits. Keeping some toys in car and allowing your Peterbald to play during these drives will also help a great deal.

Dealing with the waiting room

One place dreaded by all animals is the waiting room at the vet's clinic. There are several unpleasant sounds like the barking of dogs, cats wailing and even the chatter of humans that increase the levels of anxiety in a cat. There are also a lot of scary scents: dogs, other cats, unknown people, antiseptic, disinfectant and so on.

Cats are, by nature, solitary animals when they are not feeling well. Regardless of whether they are well, sick, relaxed or stressed they don't like being introduced to so many strange sights and sounds at once. In addition, your Peterbald is a sensitive, intuitive animal that will pick up fear in the other animals there. Animals can also discern ill health and pain in each other. The best thing to do would be to leave your cat in the carrier till he or she is called in for examination. This gives him a secure hide out and he will be less anxious or frightened.

Make sure that the carrier that you are using is large enough. Place a nice cat bed or a cushion inside for him or her to rest on. A top loading carrier is a must as it will become impossible for you to get your frightened kitty out of a front loading one.

Special pheromone sprays are available to reduce anxiety and stress in cats during their visit to the vet. These sprays imitate the scent that cats leave when they rub themselves against the legs of their loved ones.

You can also schedule your more routine vet appointments to the less busy parts of the day. That way, the chaos in the waiting room will be reduced, making your cat feel more relaxed.

Get friendly with your vet

It is good to allow your vet to spend some time with your cat and break the ice. A good vet will take a few minutes to soothe a cat patient, get to know him or her and will give your Peterbald a chance to sniff his or her coat and hands, for example.

Of course, the vet is going to have to poke and prod the cat during the examination. However, this becomes less stressful if the cat can look at the vet as a friend rather a stranger. Make sure you clear up all queries related to your cat's wellbeing when you visit your vet.

Send items from home

If your cat is scheduled for overnight hospital care or going to be admitted as a result of illness or injury, it can help if you send its favourite items such as a blanket and a toy from home. The idea is to keep him or her around familiar scents as this should help to reduce anxiety levels.

Being kept at the vet can be extremely stressful for your cat because of the noise, scents and general atmosphere. This is of course over and above any pain or sickness the cat might be feeling or experiencing. Making regular visits and sending your Peterbald things from home can really help overcome or at least diminish this anxiety. However, in some situations the vet may prohibit these items for hygiene purposes or if a vet thinks visits could just confuse and / or distress your cat.

You must always work with you vet to ensure the complete well-being of your cat. You must be able to trust the knowledge and expertise of your vet if you want him or her to be the best caregiver for your cat. Usually, vets will be more than willing to lend support in the form of information or study material to help you understand how you can take care of your cat at home.

3) Vaccinations

There is a range of vaccines for cats. They are placed into two groups: core and noncore.

The core vaccines protect against rabies, distemper, feline viral rhinotracheitis and feline calicivirus. These vaccines are given approximately every 3 years but more often in high risk areas. As with so much else, your vet will be your best guide.

Noncore vaccines are used based on a variety of factors such as breed, age, health status, the risk of exposure to certain diseases and how common a disease is in that area. In many instances cat associations recommend against these vaccines, such as the FeLV vaccine for feline leukemia. This is especially true for indoor cats.

The core vaccination timetable is:

- 6 – 7 weeks: Combination vaccine
- 10 weeks: Combination vaccine (distemper, rhinotracheitis and calicivirus) and Chlamydophila if necessary
- 12 weeks and older (governed by local laws): Rabies
- 13 weeks: Combination vaccine (distemper, rhinotracheitis and calicivirus) and Chlamydophila and Feline Leukemia if the kitten is at risk of exposure.
- 16 and 19 weeks: Combination vaccine (distemper, rhinotracheitis, and calicivirus) and Feline Leukemia if the kitten is at risk of exposure

> Adult cats: Combination vaccine (distemper, rhinotracheitis and calicivirus) and Chlamydophila and Feline Leukemia if the cat is at risk of exposure.

If you acquired your kitten or cat from a breeder the initial vaccinations will already have been done. It is vital that you keep up with them, particularly if your cat will be exposed to other cats or you live in a high risk area.

4) Neutering and spaying

As far as many are concerned, unless you are planning to breed with your Peterbald you should have your cat spayed or neutered.

Spaying is the surgical removal of the ovaries and uterus of a female cat. Neutering or castration is the surgical removal of the testicles from male cats. The hospitalization is brief, recovery is quick and the health and behavioural benefits last a lifetime!

The advantages for female cats are that they are far less likely to get breast cancer and will of course not contract uterine infections. In addition, they will no longer go into heat and indulge in activities like urinating and yowling to attract mates. This will help your pocket and your home.

With male cats, neutering prevents testicular cancer and means that your cat is far less likely to roam and therefore less likely to get into fights with other cats, be attacked by dogs or hit by a car.

In addition, the world has enough unwanted and homeless kittens. You don't want to have to home kittens that your Peterbald produced after a minute or two of fun with the scruffy tabby next door! As a pet owner one must take responsibility for the reproductive behaviour of one's pet.

To burst other myths, spaying and neutering will not make your cat fat, frustrated, crazed or depressed. Having this done is good for the cat, for you and for the community.

Best time for spaying

Peterbald cats should ideally be spayed when they are 6-9 months old. In most shelters, this is the age when the Peterbald is neutered or spayed before they are sent out for adoption.

To reduce the chances of aggression and also pregnancies, make sure you schedule to have your Peterbald spayed or neutered before it begins to mark its territory. This is when you know that your cat is physically ready to find a mate. It you have a female cat at home you must have her spayed to avoid any chance of pregnancy.

In case you have neglected spaying or neutering, you can even take your cat to the vet when he or she is in heat. However, with female cats, spaying when they are in heat will lead to excessive blood loss. If you think that you want your adult cat to be neutered or spayed, you can consult your vet about the timing and safety of the procedure.

Behaviour changes after neutering or spaying

There is no apparent permanent change in a cat's personality after neutering or spaying. It is true that the cat might be quiet and calm and not too playful for a while but he or she will get back to their usual self as soon as he or she recovers from the procedure. However, neutered males generally are less prone to roam and get into fights.

There are several myths that a Peterbald will become lethargic or obese after neutering or spaying. This puts some people off having this important procedure done. You may have to provide your cat with a certain diet after neutering or spaying. This is to ensure that the cat gets all the nutrients and calories required during the recovery process.

Chapter 9: Your Peterbald's health

If you have any concerns about the process of neutering or spaying, your vet will be able to provide you with all the necessary details.

5) General early signs of illness

Naturally the sooner you realise that your Peterbald is not well the better as your cat will suffer less and treatment is more likely to be effective.

As you get to know your Peterbald it will become increasingly easy for you to see when he or she is not well. Don't be concerned if your cat seems little off-colour for a day because that's fairly normal, but if the symptoms persist for two or more days then you need to take action. Obviously if the symptoms are dramatic or your cat has suffered an injury you need to take it to the vet immediately!

Behavioural changes to watch out for that can be very good indicators of poor health include:

- Marked increase or decrease in appetite
- Extreme tiredness or lethargy
- Difficulty in standing or moving around
- Drinking far more water than usual
- Swelling or bloating
- Atypical behaviour such as aggression
- Difficulty with defecation or urination
- Incontinence
- Discharge from the nose, ears, eyes or any body opening
- Excessive licking, scratching or biting at a part of the body.

Signs that your Peterbald is in pain include crying, tilting or shaking their head in the event of ear pain, constant licking, limping or dragging a limb, crying or even a hissing if the painful area is touched, rubbing or pawing at an eye and mouth pain may cause increased salivation.

6) Common cat illnesses and health problems

Vomiting

Vomiting is a very common feline disorder. Usually cats vomit when they consume something that disagrees with them, is poisonous to some degree or an object that is not digestible. In addition to these situations, it can also be a symptom of some form of infection, diabetes or even a urinary tract disease.

Feline lower urinary tract infection

Almost 10% of cats get affected at same stage in their lives by feline lower urinary tract infections. There are multiple causes for this group of disorders that affects both male and female cats. Most often it is stress related. In other cases, cats that eat fried foods might suffer from this condition. Feline lower urinary tract disorders are especially common in cats that are generally unhealthy, overweight or getting elderly.

The symptoms for feline lower urinary tract disorder include:

- The cat strains when urinating
- There are traces of blood in the urine
- The cat urinates in unusual places or has accidents
- Loud purrs or cries while urinating
- Constant licking in the urinary area to reduce the pain
- Depression
- Sudden Dehydration
- Loss of appetite
- Constant vomiting.

The treatment for feline lower urinary tract infection depends on the cause and the type and degree of infection. The inability to urinate is a matter of great concern. You must call your vet immediately if you observe one or more of the above symptoms.

Tapeworms

An internal infestation by tapeworms can be hazardous to your cat's health. These parasites usually invade the intestines of cats and can grow up to 2 feet in length if left untreated. Tapeworm infections have very subtle symptoms. This is why you must always keep a close watch on your cat to ensure that the problem of tapeworms does not go undetected. The symptoms include sudden weight loss even though the cat is eating, chronic vomiting and the presence of small white worms in the faeces and in the anal region.

The last symptom is an almost certain indication that a cat is infected by tapeworms. This problem is usually linked with the presence of fleas on a cat because ingesting a flea can result in an infestation by tapeworms. It is important to handle fleas as well when you are tackling the issue of tapeworms so it does not reoccur.

The most common modes of treatment include tropical medication, oral medicines and injections. Fortunately hairless Peterbald cats are far less flea prone and fleas are easier to see in less dense coats. However, you still need to be vigilant if you have a dog or cat with hair in the house.

Diarrhoea

Just as with other gastric upsets, there are several possible reasons for cats to develop diarrhoea. They range from those that are not a cause for real concern to serious conditions. The most common causes include a diet that is too rich, eating spoiled food, liver disease, allergies or food sensitivity such as lactose intolerance or cancer.

The biggest problem with diarrhoea is the danger of dehydration. It is therefore essential to give your cat plenty of fresh, clean water to drink to prevent this. Dehydration can lead to kidney and other complications that can be fatal if left untreated for two long.

You must also reduce the quantity of food you give to your Peterbald for about 24 hours.

If the diarrhoea continues and is accompanied by a loss of appetite, lethargy, bloody stools and a fever you must take your cat to the vet for examination and treatment as a matter of urgency.

Constipation

This is the most common digestive problem in domestic cats. A healthy cat will have a single, normal bowel movement a day. If your cat is constipated there is either a problem with its diet or there could be a more serious underlying health problem. Peterbald cats that are more prone to constipation include overweight cats, elderly cats and those that have a low fibre diet and insufficient exercise.

Signs to watch out for include straining and crying when eliminating or trying to do so; small, dry and hard stools; stools that are covered in mucous or blood; frequent and unproductive trips to the litter box; loss of appetite; vomiting; weight loss; lethargy; signs of abdominal discomfort such as constant licking of their tummy; and a lack of general grooming. These are all indicators of a serious case of constipation and you need to consult a vet.

The causes of constipation include factors such as dehydration or insufficient fibre in the diet, an enlarged prostate gland in male cats, a blockage or abscess in the anal sacs, a side effect of a medication, a tumour or other obstruction in the intestine, an abnormality in the colon itself, diabetes, a hernia, obesity or a foreign object the cat swallowed that is causing a blockage.

Treatment will of course be determined by the cause of the cat's constipation. However, for more routine constipation there are a number of stool softening and laxative products available for cats that are usually effective and easy to administer. Your vet may recommend a high-fibre diet for your Peterbald and / or an increase in water consumption and in exercise.

In very severe cases your vet may have to perform an enema to flush out the colon or even perform a manual evacuation of the bowels. In the event of a tumour, hernia, obstruction or malformation surgery will be required in order to either correct the problem or remove the mass that is causing the obstruction or blockage.

Eye Problems

All cats have the potential to suffer from eye problems. The most common include conjunctivitis, retinal infections, bacterial and viral infections. Glaucoma and cataracts are age related eye problems that need to be taken care of as early as possible to preserve your cat's eye sight for as long as possible.

Common symptoms of an eye problem are:

- Cloudiness in the eye or eyes
- Redness of the eyelid linings
- Eyes that are watery
- Discharge from the eye or eyes
- Pawing at or rubbing the eye; this indicates pain or itching
- Squinting
- Keeping the eye closed or the inability to open it.

Standard preliminary treatments that you can administer include flushing the eye with clean, preferably boiled and then cooled, water or a very mild saline solution and wiping away any deposits in the corner of the eye. If the problem continues, it is time to consult your vet.

Cats might also suffer injuries such as scratches to the eye if they are outdoors or have been in a fight. While very small scratches will heal on their own, marked or more serious eye injuries must be treated immediately! Peterbalds, thanks to their very fast metabolisms, heal from scratches and other wounds faster than other breeds.

Skin Problems

The hairless skin or thin coat of the Peterbald makes them more prone to some skin conditions than their dense coated or furry counterparts. This is particularly the case with regards to substances – including chemicals – their bare and sensitive skins come into contact with.
The lack of hair or dense hair, however, does also mean that it is easier for you to spot a skin problem as it will be visible. If your kitten or cat develops a rash of small red dots or lumps on the skin it might be that he or she has had an allergic reaction to something. Your Peterbald could be having a reaction to a wide range of things but the usual culprits are:

- Bacteria: your vet can identify the type involved and treat the infection easily
- Clothing: if your cat wears an item of clothing for too long it can develop a rash that then becomes infected. Your cat should not wear any item for longer than 8 hours
- Flea bites: there are various products available to deal with fleas
- Ear mites: these can be found on the body too, especially in kittens. A definitive diagnosis should be done by a vet
- Food or diet: like people, some cats are allergic to certain foods or ingredients
- Shampoo, oils or lotions: you could try hypoallergenic or non-allergenic products designed for human babies
- New medication: if this is the case your vet may be able to use an alternative
- Water or food bowls or dishes: some cats react badly to plastic. You could change to stainless steel, glass or ceramic containers

- o Household cleaning products: if a cat comes into contact with one of these it will irritate and inflame the skin. If the reaction is severe, take your cat to the vet. Alternatively wash the affected area gently and use a soothing lotion
- o New or different cat litter: cats quite often react badly to litters that are either perfumed or contain a lot of dust that is stirred up when the cat digs in the litter
- o Burns and heat rash: these can be caused by sources of heat, chemicals or overexposure to sun. If the burn is severe, take your cat to the vet immediately for pain relief and to prevent infection.

You can't protect your Peterbald from all potential allergens. Also, you won't know what he or she is allergic to until they come into contact with it and have a reaction. All a loving cat owner can do is take precautions to prevent or at least limit exposure to possible allergens and then take the right steps if a cat does have a bad reaction to something.

7) More serious conditions

Feline ectodermal dysplasia

Feline ectodermal dysplasia is a genetic disorder that Peterbalds specifically are prone to. This condition affects the lacrimal glands or the tear ducts, the teeth and the skin. It can result in a range of congenital abnormalities including missing and / or malformed teeth, decreased production of tears to moisturise and clean the eyes and a susceptibility to lung infections.

There is sadly no cure for this genetic condition. Treatment is symptomatic, such as drops to help lubricate and clean the eyes, or medicine to treat a lung infection. The extent of dental malformation will determine what can or should be done so that the cat can eat.

Cats who suffer from this condition must be spayed or castrated and should not be allowed to breed as they may pass the gene to their offspring.

Hypertrophic Cardiomyopathy

A cat's heart consists of four chambers: the left and right aorta and the left and right ventricles. It is the job of the left ventricle to receive and pump oxygenated blood to various parts of the cat's body. In the case of hypertrophic cardiomyopathy, there is a problem with the left ventricle and its ability to pump blood to the upper chamber of the heart or the aorta.

The workload on the left ventricle is a lot higher than the right ventricle. As a result, the thickness of the muscle wall in the left ventricle is greater than the right ventricle. This is common with a normally functioning heart. In cats that have Hypertrophic Cardiomyopathy, however, this thickness is abnormally marked.

Usually, this issue condition occurs in cats in the age group of 5-7 years. However, there have been reports of cats as young as 3 months developing this illness. Furthermore it is more common in male than in female cats.

If you are concerned about the state of your cat's cardiac system, or a breeder cautioned you about Hypertrophic Cardiomyopathy in your Peterbald, take him or her to the vet for an examination. The symptoms of this condition are:

- Sluggishness and lethargy
- Loss of appetite
- Shortness of breath
- Weak pulse
- Galloping rhythm, heart murmurs and other abnormal heart sounds
- Hind limb paralysis and cold paws and toes because of a clot in the aorta

- Discoloration of nail beds and footpads due to lack of oxygen flow
- Sudden collapse
- Sudden heart failure.

In addition to the genetic factors, there may be several other contributing factors that lead to Hypertrophic Cardiomyopathy. However, there is no agreement or definitive view on the causes of this serious condition yet. Experts do believe, though, that stress and hypertension can contribute and worsen an existing condition.

It is therefore important to treat stress in your cat as it occurs, and if you observe any of the symptoms listed above in him or her you need to take your Peterbald to a vet as soon as possible for accurate assessment, diagnosis and treatment.

The first thing that a vet will ask for when you take your Peterbald for an examination is his or her medical history. This includes details like the onset of the symptoms and also specific genetic information about your cat. Several procedures are used in the diagnosis of Hypertrophic Cardiomyopathy.

The first of these is the Electrocardiogram or ECG. The purpose of an electrocardiogram is to check the electrical currents in the heart. In case of any abnormality, the electric currents in the heart will be clearly different. Your vet will be able to examine the origin of these abnormal patterns in the rhythm of the heart.

If an ECG is inadequate your vet will also use radiography and / or ultrasound to determine the presence of any abnormality in the heart. These processes help create an image of the ventricles and the aorta. The vet can visually check for any abnormality in the structure of the aorta or the valves of the heart. In the case of Hypertrophic Cardiomyopathy, the valve between the left ventricle and aorta, known as the mitral valve, may also have deformities that become evident in these tests.

These tests are absolutely mandatory to ensure that your Peterbald does not have some other condition that very closely mimics Hypertrophic Cardiomyopathy. Your vet must also check your cat's blood pressure to ensure that it is not just hypertension that is causing these symptoms.

In addition, there is also a chance of hyperthyroidism which is caused by an increase in the thyroid hormone in the body of your pet. These two conditions have very similar symptoms like irregular heart rhythm, sluggishness and lethargy and need to be ruled out before assuming that your cat has Hypertrophic Cardiomyopathy. Once a firm diagnosis of Hypertrophic Cardiomyopathy has been made, it will become necessary to put your cat into hospital care, especially if the cat has congestive heart failure. The amount of stress on your Peterbald will have to be reduced drastically to ensure that there is no worsening of the condition.

If breathing is abnormal, oxygen might also be required to control the breathing and oxygen intake. Sometimes the temperature of the cat's body might fall dramatically which is particularly problematic. Blankets and warmers must be used to raise and maintain the cat's body temperature. There are several prescribed medicines that can be used to treat this condition including:

- o Diltiazim: This medicine is effective in regulating the heartbeat. In some cases, this medicine also reduces the enlargement of the ventricle.
- o Beta blockers: These are used as a measure to control irregular heartbeats. They are also corrective in nature as they help to reduce or lower the heart rate as required. In case there is a blockage of blood flow, beta blockers will take care of it.
- o Ace Inhibitors: These medicines are primarily used in cats that have congestive heart failure. They are very useful in improving the flow of blood.

- Warfarin: In case of any chances of blood clot, this medicine is recommended as it thins the blood thereby breaking down clots and reducing the chances of developing new clots.
- Aspirin: This is used to control the possibility of any blood clot and is a less aggressive medicine than Warfarin and with fewer side effects and dangers.
- Furosemide: This removes any excess water or fluid in the body that may place additional strain on the heart.
- Spironolactone: This is another medicine used specifically for cats with congestive heart failure. It is a diuretic that has is prescribed along with furosemide.
- Nitro-glycerine ointment: This ointment is necessary to dilate the ventricles and arteries.

If your Peterbald does have Hypertrophic Cardiomyopathy there are steps and precautions you can take to ensure that the symptoms don't recur.

Firstly, you will need to place your Peterbald on a strict diet. This is necessary the keep its blood pressure and weight under control. Obesity places an additional strain on the heart and this, for a cat with Hypertrophic Cardiomyopathy, could be fatal.

Secondly, you need to keep your cat quiet and away from other people, pets and children so that it won't get stressed or over-excited. If the cat gets anxious, stressed or excited there is strain on the left ventricle which exposes it to the risk of heart failure.

Finally, keep a close watch on your Peterbald during the recovery or recuperation period. There are some signs and symptoms that you must watch for as they might indicate a relapse: lethargy, trouble breathing and any weakness or paralysis of the hind limbs. It is also recommended that a cat suffering from Hypertrophic Cardiomyopathy should have an ultrasound examination six months after the recovery phase to check for progress.

Hereditary Myopathy

This nasty neurological disease, which is like a form of spasticity, is fortunately fairly rare. Breeds that have a tendency to develop the illness include the Devon Rex.

The symptoms usually become apparent in cats when they are still very young: anywhere from 3 weeks to 6 months of age. Both males and females can be affected. The severity of the disease varies between cats, and may be static or slowly progressive. Cats with this condition will suffer from:

- Muscular weakness in most muscles
- Very weak head and neck muscles
- Protruding shoulder blades
- A walk in which the front legs are lifted higher than needed
- In ability to exercise without it causing the head to bob, the stride to become increasingly short, the muscles to tremble and the cat to collapse
- When sitting, these cats often rest their front paws on a raised object
- There may be regurgitation of food and even aspiration pneumonia when food particles get into the lungs and cause infection
- The difficulty with keeping the head in a normal position may result in spasms in the larynx and throat. This is the most usual cause of death in these cats.

All of these symptoms are often worsened by urination, stress, defecation, stress, other illness, cold temperatures, or even excitement.

Sadly, there is no treatment for Hereditary Myopathy. There is usually deterioration up to 6-9 months of age. After that the disease is usually stable or only slowly progressive. The course of the disease will depend on the severity of the symptoms.

Feline Infectious Peritonitis (FIP)

FIP is caused by infection of a cat by the Feline Coronavirus virus which is very common in cats. However, often the only symptom will be mild diarrhoea. However, in rare cases the virus mutates and causes Feline Infectious Peritonitis. 80% of cats who contract FIP are younger than 2 years old.

Once a cat is infected, the virus spreads throughout the body and causes a range of symptoms including peritonitis which is an accumulation of fluid in the abdomen. In some cases the fluid gathers in the chest cavity not the abdomen. In other cats the brain, eyes, liver, kidneys or other organs become inflamed.

Ordinarily, this virus mainly infects the intestinal tract, where it thrives and then replicates or multiplies. The virus is shed in the faeces and may survive in the outside environment for several days or even a few weeks. However, it is destroyed by common disinfectants. Infection is caused when a cat ingests the virus when grooming. Some cats will always be infected but they become immune to the virus. Other cats will become infected, recover and then be re-infected. In the majority of cases there will be no symptoms other than mild diarrhoea.

FIP is a very serious complication of a Feline Coronavirus infection. In this situation the virus no longer stays in the digestive tract; it mutates and spreads throughout the body. What is difficult is that none of the symptoms a cat will exhibit are unique to FIP. Early signs, for example, include lack of appetite, lethargy and a fluctuating fever. It can take anywhere from a few days to several months before other symptoms appear.

There are two forms of FIP: 'wet' or 'effusive' disease and 'dry' or 'non-effusive' disease. Cats often have a mix of these two types. With 'wet' FIP fluid collects in the abdominal or chest cavity. This results in distension and breathing difficulty respectively. The liquid that collects is due to damaged and inflamed blood vessels that leak fluid. 'Dry' FIP usually causes chronic lesions around blood vessels in various parts of the body which lead to a type of inflammation. This inflammation can affect the eyes; the brain; tissues in the liver, kidneys, lungs and skin and even neurological disease.

Because symptoms are not unique to the disease, diagnosis is done on the basis of these symptoms and a battery of blood tests that look at white blood cell counts, protein levels in the blood, signs of jaundice or liver problems and liver enzyme levels. Often some of the fluid collecting in the abdomen or chest is analysed too. A vet may also take X-rays or an ultrasound to assess fluid collection. Only if a combination of all these symptoms and results are found can a diagnosis be made. Another diagnostic option is a biopsy of affected tissue to examine it for the Feline Coronavirus virus itself. However, a cat is usually too sick for a procedure as invasive as this.

The disease is rapid and progressive. There is no cure for FIP and not much that can be done to ease the cat's suffering other than the use of anti-inflammatory drugs. Usually euthanasia is the most humane course of action to avoid suffering.

There is a vaccine that is available in some countries to help protect against FIP that can be given to kittens over 16 weeks of age. This vaccination is especially important in breeding households or where there are large groups of cats.

Feline Leukaemia Virus (FeLV)

Amongst cats in general, Feline leukaemia virus is the second leading cause of death with the lead cause being trauma. This virus commonly causes anaemia (low red blood cells) or lymphoma (a group of blood cell tumours). It also suppresses the immune system which leaves cats open to a host of infections. The good news is that about 70% of cats who contract Feline leukaemia survive.

Transmission is through saliva, blood, urine and faeces to a lesser degree. It is therefore most often spread during grooming or if an infected cat gets into a fight. It is *not* transmitted to people or dogs. Kittens can contract the virus before birth from an infected mother or after birth from her milk. Older cats are less likely to be infected; for some reason resistance increases with age. Indoor cats are far less likely to contract the virus.
The symptoms of Feline leukaemia include appetite and weight loss, diarrhoea, pale gums or yellowish colour in the mouth and eyes, fever, breathing problems, swollen glands, infections (skin, bladder or upper respiratory tract) and unsprayed females can become sterile.

This disease is diagnosed through a blood test, called ELISA, which is done by a vet. The test looks for FeLV proteins in the blood and is able to pick infection up in the early stages. The IFA blood test is used to detect the illness if it is at the advanced stage. If the result of this test is positive for the virus the outlook or prognosis for the infected cat is not good.

Unfortunately, 85% of the cats that suffer from a persistent FeLV infection will not survive for longer than 3 years. But, regular vet visits, care and good nutrition to provide them with a good quality of life and guard against any secondary infections. These cats, though, must be kept indoors and spayed or neutered if they have not already been sterilised.

As you will have gathered, there is no cure for FeLV. Treatment is supportive and used to improve quality of life and fight secondary infections.

Feline Immunodeficiency Virus (FIV)

This virus is a complex retrovirus that leads to immunodeficiency disease in cats. In other words, cats infected with this virus can't develop or maintain a normal immune response to protect themselves from infections.

This virus, which belongs to the same class as HIV that affects people, is a slow moving virus. It can also lie dormant in the cat's body for some time before there are any symptoms. Diagnosis is usually made when a cat is about 5 years old. The likelihood of infection increases with age. Males that roam are also more likely to be infected than males that don't and females. A cat can become infected through bites and scratches from an infected cat, in utero or when suckling from an infected mother, and – far less commonly – during sexual contact as the virus has been detected in semen.

The symptoms of FIV are diverse and can be confused with those for other illnesses. For instance, some of the infections these cats get are similar to those suffered by cats with Feline leukaemia virus. Recurring minor gastrointestinal and upper respiratory tract problems are common as are swollen or enlarged lymph nodes or glands. There can also be inflammation of the gums, especially the area of tissue immediately around the teeth.

In more advanced cases there is upper respiratory tract disease and marked inflammation of various tissues including the eye, cornea, nose, glaucoma (increased pressure within the eyeball), persistent diarrhoea, chronic kidney problems and fungal infections affecting the cat's skin and / or ears. There is also usually fever and, as the disease progresses, marked weight loss. Certain types of cancers can develop, particularly in the lymphatic system, and changes to the nervous system can result in disrupted sleep and behaviour patterns, increased aggression in some cats, loss of hearing and disorders that affect the nerves in the cat's legs and feet.

Diagnosis of FIV is achieved by taking a detailed medical history, doing a thorough examination, blood tests including a blood profile and count and analysing the cat's urine. Before a final diagnosis is made, a vet must rule our parasites, tumours and infections caused by bacteria, fungi or other viruses.

Treatment of a cat with Feline immunodeficiency virus takes place on an outpatient basis unless the cat is dangerously dehydrated. The first job for the vet is to deal with secondary infections before they become serious or cause complications. If necessary, surgery is done to remove tumours and badly infected teeth. Cats living with this illness will also be placed on a specifically formulated diet.

As an owner of a cat with FIV one needs to watch one's cat for recurring or additional secondary infections or any other symptoms. A cat must also be kept on its special diet and seen regularly by a vet. If the diagnosis is made fairly early, cats with this illness can live long and relatively healthy lives.

The main focus of prevention is a vaccination. In addition to this keeping your cat indoors and away from cats that are or may be infected is the second line of defence.

8) Obesity in Peterbald cats

In case of medium sized cats like the Peterbald, the effect of being overweight or obese on their health and general well-being is always negative. Besides the usual problems like sluggishness and lethargy, obesity in cats has several associated health disorders.

Peterbald cats are mainly indoor cats. This means that they need constant stimulation to keep them active. If your cat is unable to get the amount of exercise that he or she requires, be prepared to deal with 'weighty' cat issues.

Sometimes it becomes very difficult to determine if your cat is overweight. Obesity is harder to miss! Just because the cat's levels of activity and agility seem to be fine doesn't mean that it is not chubbier than it should be. There are reliable ways of telling if your cat is becoming obese. You can try three simple tests at home before you have an actual expert test your cat for obesity.

How to tell if your Peterbald is overweight

Step number one is to feel the area around the rib cage of your cat. If you are still able to feel the rib cage easily, it means that he or she is not obese. However, if you have to press really hard to get to his rib cage, it means that your cat is heavier than the normal, acceptable weight.

Secondly, a cat's waistline has a distinct shape. The body tapers from the belly towards the hind quarters. If it is too tubby and extends evenly from belly to the rear quarters and pelvis, it is a sign that your cat needs to lose weight.

A hanging pouch between the hind legs of a cat is a definite indication of the cat being overweight. If the pouch is more like a flap of skin rather than a fat-filled pouch it probably means that your older cat was too fat, lost the weight but the skin had stretched.

Like humans, cats that are overweight will experience several health issues. Therefore, you must take necessary measures to slim your cat down and maintain a healthy weight.

Obesity related health problems

One of the most common complaints in veterinary clinics across the world is health disorders related to obesity. One of the biggest threats to the well-being of cats is feline diabetes mellitus. The second most prevalent disorder in cats due to obesity is hyperthyroidism which is due to excessive production of thyroid.

According to experts, the chances of an obese cat becoming diabetic are double in comparison to cats that have a normal weight. This risk becomes 8 times higher if the cat becomes severely obese. The association between obesity and diabetes is quite evident. When your cat becomes obese, there is a drastic increase in the amount of inflammatory markers and oxidative stress. This causes insulin resistance which leads to obesity.

The resistance to insulin is one of the most common problems found in cats. It has also been observed that a change in diet is not as effective in increasing insulin sensitivity as the actual reduction in weight. There are several other health conditions that can be found in cats due to feline obesity.

Osteoarthritis and lameness: This condition occurs because there is too much stress on the medium sized frame of your Peterbald. You will be able to hear loud thuds when your cat jumps off a table or chair which indicates a gradual loss of agility in the cat.

Liver and urinary system: Too much pressure on the liver also causes liver problems like feline lipidosis syndrome. Also, urinary tract disorders are common in cats that are obese.

The biggest issue with obesity is not the condition itself. The inability of many owners to recognize this condition and provide necessary treatment is the cause for the drastic increase in feline obesity in the last couple of years. There are many cases that have been reported where owners are just used to over-feeding their cat. They actually think a normal sized cat looks malnourished and unhealthy.

As the owner, it is your responsibility to evaluate the condition of your cat's body on a regular basis. You can also get a body condition score card to check for the amount of fat present in your cat's body. These scores show the difference in the calorie intake of your cat and the actual energy requirement. If your Peterbald is being overfed, the score will increase to indicate an increase in fat deposits.

How to keep your Peterbald at a healthy weight

It is actually not very difficult to maintain your cat's normal body weight. All you need to do is ensure that the width of the hips and shoulders are maintained without any visible bulge on the sides. You must also make sure that the belly of your cat does not hang too low.

Since the Peterbald is a hairless or near-hairless and a slender cat by nature, fat deposits become very evident early on. There are a few things you can do to reduce obesity in your cat.

Understand what the right amount of food is: The amount of food that you give your cat should be just enough to keep it healthy. It is impossible here to quantify the food that you should give to your Peterbald. However, you can measure the calorie intake in your cat. Your vet or a local breeder or association can advise you as to how many kilocalories per kilo of body weight your cat should be getting given its breed, age and gender.

Depending on your cat's health, you can determine how much food it requires. If there has been any recent surgical procedure or neutering / spaying, you must make sure you reduce the food intake accordingly.

Free choice feeding is a very common problem. Cat owners, out of love, provide their cat with a range of flavours and choices leading to over-eating. If you mix dry cat food with canned food there is a chance of overeating. Similarly, constant changes in the taste of foods will make your cat overeat because of the novelty. Like us, cats find it hard to resist a great tasting meal.

Using a measuring cup to judge portion size and so ensure that your cat is neither over fed nor under fed can be very helpful. However, if you prefer free choice feeding, divide the food into two portions. Give your cat one helping in the morning and one in the evening. You must also be very careful that the food is age appropriate. Depending on whether you have a kitten or a senior cat in your household, the choice of diet will vary.

The importance of keeping your cat hydrated can't be stressed enough. You must make sure that there is plenty of fresh water

Chapter 9: Your Peterbald's health

available for your cat, especially if you are feeding it dry cat food, While most dry foods work very well for cats, lack of water might lead to issues like urinary tract disorders and also lowered kidney function.

Water is an essential nutrient for your Peterbald. Irrespective of whether you are feeding it wet or dry food, you must give it enough water. The presence of adequate amounts of water in the body will help your cat process and absorb the food that it has eaten. Proper digestion and elimination, which is the key to good health in a cat, is regulated by the amount of water available.

If you have put your cat on a weight loss diet, you must give him or her adequate amounts of protein. It is true that the calorie intake must be restricted. However, you must always make sure that you do not reduce the amount of essential nutrients. When you increase the amount of proteins, weight loss is aided while keeping the lean body mass intact.

If you are concerned about the weight and health of your Peterbald, make sure you reduce the amount of treats and titbits. This practice must be extended to at least a couple of weeks after the official 'diet' period. You must make sure that everyone in your family is aware of this rule. If you try and cheat out of affection, remember that you are harming your cat's health. It would help, instead, to cut your cat's meals down to smaller, more frequent ones. This will ensure that it does not experience hunger pangs while continuing to stay on a healthy diet.

Crash diets are as harmful for cats and they are for humans. You must never starve your cat. In fact, no matter what restrictions you make in its diet, it must be supervised by a vet or dietician. If you don't carefully monitor the amount of minerals and vitamins your cat is getting it can lead to a fatal condition called hepatic lipidosis which affects the liver.

Exercise is extremely important in cats. You cannot control the health and weight of your Peterbald by only altering its diet. You must ensure that it has an active lifestyle. This means that you will be both controlling the calories your cat takes in and making sure that he or she burns the calories through exercise and activity. One can do a number of things to encourage activity and to keep your cat's environment stimulating and engaging.

To begin with, set aside a dedicated time to play with your cat or cats. You can use simple toys like strings to help your Peterbald play and get a good workout. (You will probably get one too!) Agility training (discussed earlier) provides a great deal of safe exercise.

In addition, allow his or her natural instincts to take over; let your cat climb, jump, pounce, scratch and even chase around the house. These exercises are interesting and fun for your cat and will increase the process of weight loss.

It is suggested that cat owners get a feeding ball to give a cat one meal in the day. The advantage with the feeding ball is that your cat will have to put in some effort to roll the ball in order to get to the food inside. Also, you could place your cat's food bowl at the top of a flight of stairs. This will encourage your Peterbald to climb to get to the food.

Throughout the process of weight loss, you must be extremely patient. It will take several weeks and even months for your cat to lose weight. If you find it too hard to maintain the weight of your cat on your own, you can ask your vet for tips. You could even enrol your Peterbald and yourself in a veterinary weight loss clinic for additional support and information.

9) How to give your Peterbald medication

Giving medication to a cat can be a challenge. One needs to try and do so in a way that will not stress or hurt your cat… or you!

In order to give your Peterbald a pill or tablet, hold it against your body and on a surface that is about waist height to you. Place the thumb and fingers of one hand on either side of your cat's mouth. If you press gently with your fingers and tilt the cat's head back, its mouth should open automatically. Using your other hand, gently pull the lower jaw down and place the pill or tablet as far back on the tongue as you can. Continue to hold the head back and keep the mouth closed until you are sure that your cat has swallowed the medication.

If you need to give a liquid medication, tip the cat's head back. Open his or her mouth as you would if you were going to be administering a pill or tablet. Then pull out a corner of the lower lip to form a pocket. Pour the liquid into the pocket and hold your cat's mouth closed until he or she has swallowed. Don't try to administer so much at once that most of the dose is spilled before it has a chance to go into the mouth.

If you need to restrain a cat, for whatever reason, wrap it in a soft blanket with only the part of the cat you need to deal with exposed.

10) How to clean your cat's teeth

Even if there are no extra dental problems caused by ectodermal dysplasia, the healthy Peterbald is susceptible to routine problems with its teeth and gums as all cats are. The most common of these is gingivitis or gum inflammation.

This condition is caused by the build up of plaque mixed with saliva and food particles on the teeth. If this hardens into tartar and builds up along the gum line the gums become inflamed and even infected. If periodontal disease goes unchecked your cat will eventually lose his or her teeth.

The vet can remove tartar by using a procedure known as descaling. However, if you practice good dental hygiene from the time your Peterbald is a kitten you can avoid any serious oral or dental diseases.

Chapter 9: Your Peterbald's health

It is very important that you begin to clean your Peterbald's teeth when he or she is still a kitten. This way your cat will be used to it even though it will never enjoy it. It is best to clean a cat's teeth daily. The absolute minimum is twice a week.

The best way to handle the dental routine is to collect all the supplies you will need in advance before you tackle your cat. Some cat owners use sterile gauze strips to clean their cat's teeth. Others begin with gauze and move, as their cat becomes more tolerant, to a soft rubber toothbrush.

You can buy toothbrushes and toothpaste from your vet. Please note that you should never under any circumstances use toothpaste that is designed for people as this could be very dangerous, even fatal, for your cat!

In order to get a kitten used they sensation of having something in its mouth, you can begin by just using your little finger which you have dipped into something the kitten will enjoy the taste of. For example, you could use the brine solution that tinned tuna comes in. Once your kitten has become used to this, begin to wrap gauze around your finger which has also been soaked in the solution the kitten will like. To begin with, only clean one or two teeth in a session and then gradually increase the number of teeth.

Dip your finger, the gauze or the toothbrush into the feline toothpaste a saline solution. With the cat on your lap, gently open its jaws using the same technique you would if you were administering medication and rub your finger or the toothbrush on each tooth using a circular motion. You need to pay particular attention to the areas next to the gum where tartar builds up. Don't rub or brush too hard or you could injure the gums and this could result in an infection.

As with all the hygiene and health care procedures you do with your cat you must remember to make comforting sounds and talk soothingly to him and her while you were working. Afterwards you need to praise him or her and make time for cuddles and even playing a game. Your cat should enjoy the rewards so much that he or she is willing to endure grooming in order to have the fun afterwards!

11) The self-medicating cat

We've all seen cats eating grass and many of us assume that it is something they do when their tummies aren't feeling quite right. All cats eat grass, but the experts are not entirely sure why.

Eating grass certainly seems to help cats that need to regurgitate hair they have swallowed. A considerable amount of grass consisting of whole blades does have an emetic effect. It is also possible that when they just nibble at the tips of grass cats are taking in roughage they feel they need in order to regulate their digestive systems. Another theory is that they get additional trace elements and vitamins from grass.

Whatever the reason, it appears that cats need and want to eat grass on occasion. If you don't have a garden or your cat is purely an indoor cat you will need to plant a window box or a pot with grass for your kitty to snack on.

12) De-clawing a cat

In a word: don't! The process of de-clawing a cat involves the surgical amputation of the first joint of every digit on the cat's front feet. In other words, it is a mutilation of the cat that causes considerable post-operative pain and possible phantom pain the rest of its life. If you train your cat properly and supply a scratching post there is absolutely no reason to do this.

This practice is followed in order to prevent the cat from damaging furniture and property. Other pet owners also justify declawing a cat as a method of protecting other people from being scratched or hurt by their cat. In some residential properties, people are not allowed to keep cats unless they are completely declawed.

It is quite certain that those who advocate declawing don't understand the seriousness of this procedure. It is not a way of keeping the nails trimmed or blunt. It is a medical surgery that has horrible repercussions for the cat. There is also no guarantee that your Peterbald will recover entirely from this traumatic experience. For this reason, several European countries have strong laws against declawing the cat. Some breeders make new owners sign an agreement saying they will never declaw the cat.

If you have considered declawing or had it suggested to you, remember that the toes and claws are an important part of the anatomy of the cat which makes it more agile and graceful. It allows it purchase on surfaces. Declawing also deprives a cat of its instinctive defence mechanism: the ability to climb a tree to escape danger at ground level and to use its claws to defend itself by scratching an attacker.

The recuperation period is very hard and painful and the short-, medium- and long-term impact on the cat is significant. For up to 3 days, the cat will suffer post procedure lameness and will drag itself around. A cat will not lose its instinctive behaviour even if it is in pain. It will therefore still need to jump and scratch despite the pain. It will also have to use the litter box. This will impact on recovery time.

Almost 80% of cats that have undergone declawing have developed complications after surgery or even after discharge that were caused by the wrong sheering techniques being used or even the nature of the blade used for surgery. The most common conditions include abscesses, necrosis (death) of tissue, growth of deformed claws, motor paralysis, nerve damage, haemorrhage, stress induced bladder inflammation, infections, swelling and even reluctance to walk.

Furthermore, there have been reports that declawing can change the cat's personality including in cats that were previously loving and gentle:

- ➢ The biting frequency and strength increases in most cats. The only possible explanation to this is that when a cat loses one form of defence, it activates or strengthens another.
- ➢ House soiling is twice as common in declawed cats. Firstly, they become reluctant to walk and put pressure on their paws. In addition, severe cases like nerve dysfunction and even lameness leave the cat helpless.
- ➢ Aggression is very common in cats post declawing. The pain makes them more defensive. Also, the fact that you, their owner, inflicted that pain on him or her makes you less trustworthy in the eyes of your cat and the cat generally less trusting and far more anxious.

Almost 45% of cats in America that have been declawed are referred to vet teaching hospitals and cat schools to sort out behavioural issues. The change in behaviour is more drastic if the cat has undergone tendonectomy in the process of being declawed. The repercussions of these behaviour changes include relinquishing cats to shelters. For a cat like the Peterbald which gets particularly attached to people, this experience is extremely traumatic.

There are alternatives to declawing a cat.

- ✓ Trim your cat's nails with a nail clipper. This will reduce the damage caused by your cat's claws to a large extent.
- ✓ Another simple option is to provide your cat with a scratching post. You can attract your cat to the scratching post by using scent sprays. A sisal scratch post is most recommended for cats as the roughness of the surface is just right for the cat to fulfil its urge to scratch something.
- ✓ One of the simplest and most effective solutions are nail caps made of vinyl that you can simply glue to the front claws of your cat. You can even protect your children from the cat with the help of products like 'Soft Claws'. Once these caps wear off, they can be simply replaced with a new set.

- ✓ Train your cat. That is the best way to protect your space and others from the claws of the cat. Teach your cat to only use the scratch post. You can also train it to be at its best behaviour when it is around strangers.

For a cat like the Peterbald, which mostly remains indoors, all the above alternatives work fine. In case your cat is in the habit of venturing outside, you might want to avoid clipping the nails or even using nail caps so that your cat can be on guard.

13) A first aid kit for your cat

First aid items for your cat should be stored in a suitable container that is accessible, portable and clearly marked. It is recommended that a feline first aid kit should include the following items:

- o Antibiotic powder
- o Antiseptic wash
- o Eye dropper
- o Gauze swabs
- o Hydrogen peroxide 3%
- o Cat laxative product
- o Roll of cotton wool or absorbent cotton
- o Roll of adhesive bandage (2.5 cm or 1" wide)
- o Roll of adhesive bandage (7.5 cm or 3" wide)
- o Roll of gauze bandage (2.5 cm or 1" wide)
- o Sharp, pointed scissors
- o Round tip scissors
- o 20 ml plastic syringe
- o Thermometer
- o Anti-bacterial and anti-fungal solution such as tincture of iodine
- o Torch or flashlight
- o Tweezers.

In order to maintain the kit, you will need to clean any instrument that you have used before putting it back in the kit. If any of the consumables are used, replace them before you forget to do so.

It is also advisable to check the kit contents every six months to ensure that everything is in order, nothing has expired and that the batteries in the torch or flashlight still work.

14) Preparing your cat for surgery

No matter what surgical procedure your cat is going to undergo, a good amount of preparation is mandatory. You can get all the necessary pre surgical advice from your vet. Make sure you adhere to all the guidelines.

The most common precaution to take is to ensure that your cat does not eat anything after midnight until the surgery. If you are taking a kitten for an operation, on the other hand, the nutritional requirements are drastically different and you should ask your vet for guidance.

Following these measures will at worst reduce the chances of complications and, at best, ensure that there are no complications during the surgery, immediately following it and later on during the recuperation phase after your Peterbald has left the animal hospital.

15) The recovery process

Your Peterbald will experience discomfort to some or other degree after the procedure. If your cat is in pain, you must make sure you either leave it under specialized care or consult your vet regularly. There are a few precautions that you can take to ensure that the recovery process is comfortable and safe.

- Give your cat a safe, quiet place in the house to rest during the recovery process. This place should not be accessible by other pets or even children.

- Do not encourage jumping, running or playing during the recovery process. You can take your Peterbald out on walks but make sure that it doesn't get physically overexerted.
- The area that has been operated on should not be licked. So, getting your cat an Elizabethan collar is the best option although the vet will probably put one on.
- During the recovery process, avoid using litter in the litter box and rather use shredded paper. The problem with sand or litter is that the dust can get into a wound and cause infections or irritation.
- The site of the incision must be cleaned regularly to avoid infections.
- Look out symptoms at the site of the incision:
  - Redness
  - Swelling in the site of the incision
  - Discharge from the area
- Reduced appetite
- Vomiting
- Lethargy.

If you do notice one or more of these symptoms, you need to inform your vet immediately.

Chapter 10: Behavioural issues

Your cat's health must be your priority. You can ensure that your Peterbald stays healthy by taking it for regular vet visits, having all the necessary vaccinations and deworming done, providing it with nutritious food and also ensuring that it gets enough exercise. Most physical health issues can be treated quite easily. However, if you see sudden behaviour changes in your cat, it could be suffering from some psychological disorder.

1) Sleeping habits

One of the things cats do best is sleep. On average, a healthy adult cat spends 16 or even more out of every 24 hours sleep. In other words, they spend two thirds of their time sleeping. Scientists and researchers are not quite sure why cats sleep so much.

Cats will have shorter naps and long sleeps throughout the day. No two cats will have the same sleep routines any more than people do. Sleep patterns are also affected by the weather, the cat's age, how relaxed it is feeling, its state of health, whether it is hungry or not and what its human companion is doing.

There is a fair amount of anecdotal evidence that suggests that cats are more likely to sleep when their people are not there or unavailable. Domestic cats often seem to adjust their sleep patterns in accordance with the daily rhythms of its owner and the household it lives in.

All cats will choose favourite sleeping spots. Often these will be in cool or shaded patches on a very hot day, somewhere warm and free of drafts on a cold day, and of course on a surface that is as comfortable and snuggly as possible. Cat owners have stopped being surprised to find their cat sleeping on a chair, a bed, in a draw on top of clothes, or somewhere else that is not necessarily terribly convenient for the owner.

Just like human beings, when cats sleep there is more than one type of sleep: there are periods of lighter sleep and others of much deeper sleep. Interestingly, EEG results indicate that in deep sleep there is almost as much brain activity in a cat is when it is awake.

As with many other mammals, there are also periods of REM or rapid eye movement sleep. This is also a state of deep sleep and usually the phase of sleep in which dreams occur. Do cats dream? That's impossible to determine. It seems possible, however.

2) Behaviour problems

There are a number of fairly common behavioural problems one encounters in cats including the Peterbald. It is certainly best to try and nip undesirable behaviours in the bud when you first start to notice them.

Missing the litter box

One of these areas of difficulty is when your kitten or adult cat starts to miss the litter box. Before looking for a more complex reason begin with the more obvious ones. For instance, is the litter box dirty? Cats are clean by nature and will not use a litter box that's dirty or too damp. Have you started using a different type of cat litter? It might be that your kitten or cat doesn't like the smell or feel of it. Cats also like their privacy. Is the litter box in a place where there is a lot of activity?

Most of the time, this behaviour can be explained by looking at these issues. Once it has been addressed the problem goes away.

Scratching

A second fairly common problem is a cat that scratches your furniture, carpets and curtains. If you don't already have a scratching post buying one must be the first thing you do. If you do have a scratching post that your cat is not using, you will have to retrain it to do so (please see chapter 6).

Chapter 10: Behavioural issues

Excessive scratching can also cause problems for a cat as it may bleed as the skin becomes raw or if a nail tears. It has been noted that cats use scratching as a tool to demand for your attention. It is best to take note of this behaviour before your Peterbald inflicts physical pain on itself.

Urinating or defecating in the house

An unfortunately common behavioural problem with cats is urination or defecation in the house. This is very difficult for cat owners in terms of knowing how to deal with their cat, cleaning up the mess and the unpleasant smells – sometimes lingering ones – that go with it.

There could be a number of reasons why your cat is doing this. With urinating, the most frequent reasons are that your cat is marking the house as his or her territory, they have a medical problem, they can't or won't use the litter box for some reason or they are stressed or frightened.

Start by taking your cat to the vet. Once you have ruled out a medical reason you can deal with the underlying cause and the behaviour should stop.

Don't shout at, smack or rub your cat's nose in it; this will just create a fearful, stressed cat and it will not stop the behaviour.

Attention seeking disorder

Cats with this problem will 'meow' nonstop at certain times of the day or night. Their constant howling can become a nuisance for the owner, family and even neighbours. One needs to try and understand what is causing a cat to behave in this manner. The howling of a cat can be broadly categorized as crying or meowing. The cause for such behaviour can be either emotional or physical pain that the cat is experiencing.

Some cats produce a truly mournful howl that sounds as though they are calling out for help. This particular howl can make the

Chapter 10: Behavioural issues

cat owner cringe with sympathy for the poor creature. It can be a result of pain, suddenly feeling lost, deafness or even a call for help from an old or infirm cat. Some cat owners think that it can also happen when a cat wakes from a bad dream.

The reason for this howl need not always be an emotional one. A certain condition called as Feline Hyperesthesia is also associated with this behaviour. When a cat howls during the night and is found rolling on the floor then you must consider this condition. It is more commonly known as Rippling Skin Disorder and is a stress related condition. However, the symptoms usually include a set of unrelated issues. The cats tend to become extremely sensitive to touch and the skin begins to show ripples.

The possible causes of this disorder are the excessive presence of unsaturated fatty acids in combination with Vitamin E deficiency, brain infection or trauma or even flea allergies. If the cat is diagnosed with this disorder then it is unlikely that it will be completely cured. So, paying attention to these issues can help you provide greater comfort to the cat and keep tabs on its behavioural issues.

Chronic pseudo hunger can also cause these distressing howls. They are not uncommon in cats. Like people, cats also have food cravings which are unwarranted. Cats tend to develop a strong liking for some treats such as tuna flakes. This can also turn into an addiction of sorts. This causes the cat to beg for food all day because of cravings that are misread as hunger.

Cats that run around their owner's feet in circles run the risk of accidentally being trodden on and making their owner fall. This is also categorized under attention seeking issues in cats. They are muck like kids who need a little bit of extra attention. They also tend to rub themselves against your arm when they need extra attention.

Cats are vocal generally and the Peterbald is more so than many breeds. They like to have conversations with their owners. Some chatty cats tend to draw their owners into lengthy conversations. If the owner doesn't spend enough time with a very sociable, chatty cat, it is likely to become lonely and stressed.

Aggression towards other cats

Many people don't get too concerned when their cats have scraps or the odd fight. An all-out fight with an outsider tends to be more dramatic and taken more seriously. However, it is wise to be watchful when your cats get into a fight because you have to make sure that it doesn't turn ugly or result in injury.

Cats fight for several reasons including fear, territorial misunderstandings, competition for a female, stress venting, anxiety, display etc. There are various kinds of aggression that are seen in cats.

Sexual aggression in cats is a common phenomenon but it is not often seen. However, when two cats get sexually aggressive towards each other, the dominant cat bites the nape of the less dominant or subservient cat's neck and then attempts to climb onto the subservient cat's back. This can be mistaken for mating behaviour.

Territorial aggression is also observed quiet often amongst all animals including domestic cats. Cats mark their territory by urinating, spraying or rubbing their faces against objects. This leaves their scent which tells other cats whose turf it is. Cats will hiss and growl to warn an intruder that he or she is unwelcome. If the intruder pays no attention to the warnings then a fight will usually take place. Fortunately, this does not occur between Peterbald cats too often as they are, as a rule, less territorial than most other breeds.

Aggression directed at human beings

It is unlikely that cats become friendly with everybody who visits your home. Most domesticated cats are civil to guests or will simply quietly leave if they are uncomfortable in the surrounding. However, when a cat tends to get aggressive towards people in general then it is a clear indication of the fact that the particular cat has been poorly trained when it was younger. Biting, scratching and unpleasant vocalization are indications of a badly trained or socialised cat. Some possible causes of aggressive cat behaviour towards human beings are:

Overstimulation: This problem surfaces when the owner of the cat or a person does not understand the body language of the cat. There are cats that enjoy petting while others prefer to be left alone. Even the most petting-friendly cats don't like to be cuddled or stroked for unreasonable lengths of time. When they get over stimulated, they tend to scratch or bite to show that their petting session is over.

If one watches a cat closely you will see that the cat starts moving away. It might begin by pulling its ears back and narrowing its eyes. If the owner fails to understand these signals then the cat begins to lash its tail. Finally, if the owner continues the cat may become aggressive and scratch or bite.

Redirected aggression comes about when the cat's aggression towards his owner or other human beings is not necessarily due to something that person has done but to something else that has frightened or disturbed the cat. For example, when your Peterbald spots a foreign cat or any other strange animal around the house there is a possibility of the cat becoming agitated and aggressive. As a reaction to this your cat will scratch or bite the first thing it can reach even if it is you.

3) Going away and travelling with your Peterbald

Whether you are going on a vacation or going on a business trip, you must make the right arrangements for your Peterbald while you are away. You need to ensure that your cat is in safe hands and is somewhere where it will be treated well and given a lot of

Chapter 10: Behavioural issues

love and affection. There are several options that are available, but the most common and the most reliable ones are:

Friends: If you are a cat lover, you will most likely be in the company of several others who feel the same way. There will definitely be someone in your group who can pitch in to take care of your cat while you are away. When you are handing this responsibility over to a friend, make sure that he or she has had pets in the past, preferably a cat. You must look for someone who will be able to make your cat comfortable and less anxious.

Family: If you have relatives who visit you regularly, leaving your cat in their care is a great idea because your cat will be familiar with their smell and sight and will be able to adjust better in their company. If someone from your family is willing to stay over at your place and take care of your cat while you are away, it is the ideal scenario.

A neighbour: If you have friendly neighbours who love cats, ask them to take care of your Peterbald. Neighbours, again, will be familiar to your cat and will therefore be able to comfort it while you are away. Not just that, the locality and the surroundings will not be too different for your cat to make adjustments to.

A pet sitter: There are several companies and a number of individuals who will be willing to provide you with pet sitting services while you are away. You can ask for recommendations from people who have used their services in the past to choose the right company or individual to care for your Peterbald.

Meet the people who work at the company or the pet sitter. If you are sure that they are gentle, kind and, most importantly, responsible, you can do a trial run for one evening. If your see that they are good with your cat and that your cat is comfortable in their presence, you can give them the responsibility of taking care of your Peterbald while you are away.

Chapter 10: Behavioural issues

A boarding home or cattery: There are several places where your cat can be boarded for the period that you are away. These professionals have all the necessary personnel. From people who feed and clean the cages to certified veterinarians, you will find that all the services are provided in these shelters. Here again you can ask for recommendations before you actually decide to place your cat in a particular cattery or kennel. Make a visit to these places to check their standards of hygiene. The conditions of the cages, the staff available and the facilities available play an important role in the decision that you make.

If you have to travel and leave your Peterbald home alone, make sure that you take all the necessary measures to schedule your trip according to your cat. Plan well in advance and keep a list of options that are available to take care of your cat. Never rush these things at the last minute because you will end up making compromises on the necessary arrangements.

One can never say when an emergency will occur. In case you have to leave suddenly, you must be able to find the best assistance for your cat's care. So, it is a good idea to make a list of people or companies who will be willing to take care of your cat. Sadly, cats are not the best travel companions. If you have had a dog for a pet, never assume that your Peterbald will be as easy to travel with. Whether you are travelling by car or train, make sure air conditioning is available to keep your cat comfortable.

Travelling by car

If you are travelling by car remember that you must never leave your cat to wander around in the car. If your cat jumps on the driver or gets under his or her feet or the pedals, the consequences could be fatal! Make sure that you always carry your cat in a carrier. The carrier should be extremely sturdy and must be made from metallic wires or even fibre glass. The carriers made from light plastic or even cardboard are not meant for long journeys. They are only suitable for short trips like a visit to the vet.

The weather that you travel in is extremely important in deciding what measures you need to take while travelling. If you think that it will get hotter as your journey proceeds, make sure that you get a carrier that allows a good amount of air circulation. In case it is going to get cold along the way, carry enough blankets to wrap your Peterbald up and keep it warm. There are also draft free carriers that will ensure that you do not leave your kitty shivering and uncomfortable.

Irrespective of the kind of carrier that you buy, there is one more thing that you need to consider. In case you are planning to change your mode of transport along the way, plane for example, you must also check for the guidelines that the transport provider uses with respect to the type of carrier that is allowed.

If you have ample space in the back of your car and you only intend to travel by car, you can even use a large crate to keep your cat in. All you need to do is place blankets and sheets inside this crate and put it in the back seat of your car. The only thing that you need to ensure is that you provide your cat with a quiet place where he can rest during the journey. Place his favourite toys and treats around him to reduce the stress of travelling. The bedding that you provide during the travelling period should be the one that he is already used to and has his pheromones on it.

Make sure that the crate or the carrier is completely secure. Even if you were to apply brakes suddenly it must be safe. If the carrier or crate falls suddenly, your cat will be startled. The last thing you want while travelling is an anxious – or even injured - cat. Finally, never place your cat in the boot of your car as this area is very dark and badly ventilated. Check on your Peterbald regularly throughout the journey and make sure that it is comfortable.

Travelling by train

When you are travelling by train, you must obviously place your cat in a carrier. Since there are strangers on a train, you do not want to have any instances of your cat breaking free and running

Chapter 10: Behavioural issues

scared or scaring the passengers. So, make sure that the carrier that you have is extremely sturdy.

The base of the carrier must be strong to ensure that your cat is secured. The carrier itself should be light so that you do not have any difficulty carrying it around. It must also be of a convenient size depending upon the space available on the train. Make sure that you get a carrier that is large enough for your cat to rest in. Never cram your Peterbald into a small carrier because there isn't enough storage space.

You must keep a familiar blanket in the carrier to reduce anxiety. However, littering and soiling can be quite a concern. So, line your cat's cage with a good amount of absorbent paper so that you both have a pleasant journey.

Travelling by Air

Travelling with your pet by air requires a good deal of planning in advance. Not all airlines are prepared to transport cats. If they do, cats are handled as freight. It is recommended that you avoid air travel where possible. However, if you do find airlines that have the facility to transport your Peterbald, you must take several precautions. For instance, don't transport a pregnant cat or a kitten less than three months of age by air.

Check for a license to transport animals in the airlines that you choose. There are is a chance that you and your cat will travel on separate flights. If this is true, make sure that you get a direct flight for your cat so that he or she does not have to deal with delays because of issues like transits and transfers.

Find out whether you need to provide proof of vaccinations and health status. Some airline companies insist that a cat that is going into the cargo hold must be sedated for the duration of the flight.

Travelling with your Peterbald can be fun if you prepare it in advance. The most important thing to do is to condition him or her to enjoy sitting inside a carrier. If you are able to accomplish this you have already won half the battle.

4) Why and how your cat purrs

It used to be believed that cats purr when they are content and happy. This is only part of what is apparently a more complex mechanism. Research now indicates that it is a means of communicating and may also be a form of self-healing.

A cat will also purr if it feels threatened or frightened. A vet by the name of Kelly Morgan has an interesting theory: a purr is the feline equivalent of a smile in people. This makes sense as people smile when happy, sometimes to hide embarrassment, to appease the other person or even to mask anger.

How a cat purrs is also interesting. A part of the brain, a neural oscillator, sends a message to the muscles of the larynx. These muscles begin to twitch incredibly fast: 25 – 150 vibrations per second. Because of the vibrations, the vocal cords separate as the cat breathes in and out. The resulting sound is a purr.

In addition to using the purr to communicate with people and other cats, bioacoustics researchers now think that purring helps cats to heal. Vibrations in the range that the vocal cords vibrate have been shown to relieve pain, heal wounds faster and even promote bone growth and density. The purring of your Peterbald could well have health and healing benefits for you too.

5) Feline stress and dealing with it

Animals also get stressed but they don't have the same range of options to relieve it that we do. Your Peterbald will lower your stress levels. You need to do the same for him or her!

Stress has its advantages because, thanks to the adrenaline it releases, it can boost performance or even help an animal, and people, avoid injury or death. It is responsible for the important

"Fight or flight" response. The danger arises when the stress is either acute or chronic; if a cat goes on feeling stressed for a long time there are numerous harmful effects.

The most significant of the physical consequences is damage to the immune system. A chronically stressed cat can loose its appetite, become agitated, urinate or defecate in the house, spray, begin to tremble or shiver, cry much more than usual, become very restless or even hide. Keep in mind though that these symptoms could also be caused be a medical condition so rule that out first.

Once you know that your Peterbald isn't sick, you need to identify the cause of the stress. Have you moved recently? Has a new pet or person been introduced into your home? Is there new furniture or have you redecorated? Are you packing to go away? Has your neighbour acquired a new pet that your cat could have had contact with? Any of these changes, or a host of others, could stress of some cats. Others will take it in their stride or find it fun!

Your first line of attack is to change the situation that is causing the problem. If that is not going to be possible you may need to consider removing the cat. For instance, if there are workmen in your home consider placing your Peterbald with a trusted friend or at a cattery until the home is back to normal.

The next option is to help your cat change its response to stress. Spend extra time with your Peterbald stroking and soothing it. Massaging cats can have a wonderfully relaxing effect on them. Stroke and speak to your cat as you slowly approach the source of stress.

Don't push too hard or rush your cat; you need to acclimatize him or her gently. If necessary you can get a sedative of some sort from the vet. In extreme cases some owners opt to consult a cat therapist or behaviourist.

Chapter 10: Behavioural issues

6) *Moving house with your cat*

Moving house with a Peterbald is easier than with many other breeds because they are less territorial than most and, so long as you are around, your cat should cope fairly well. However, there are still things that you need to do – or not do – to make a move as non stressful as possible.

If you are just moving a short distance, say within the same city or town, you need to move your belongings and set up your new home first before you move your cat. That way you can arrive with your cat in its carrier and introduce it to the new house with the familiar furniture already in place.

However, if you are moving a longer distance you will transport your cat in your car or on a train or plane as discussed and described in detail earlier in this chapter. If you are still arranging furniture or the movers are still moving in and out of the premises when you arrive, you must spare your Peterbald all of the commotion and upheaval.

Find a quiet, safe room in the new house where you can put him or her. Leave the carrier, a blanket, food, water and a litter box in the room. Keep the door closed or locked so he or she won't be bothered or accidently let out of the room. Remember to visit your cat regularly and make some time to pet and talk to it. When you move into a new home you need to keep your Peterbald inside even if ordinarily he or she was allowed outside at times at your previous home. This is a new and therefore unknown and scary environment for your cat. A real danger can be if a cat gets a fright or becomes alarmed, and it is not yet familiar with its surroundings, it can run and either get lost or get into trouble in the form of other animals or traffic in nearby roads. Your cat must, even if only initially, be a purely inside cat until you are sure that he or she is settled.

Chapter 10: Behavioural issues

Of course there will be some variation. Some cats will settle fast and will be able – and want – to explore the whole house from the start. Others will need a room or a hiding place in which to settle and they will venture out for short exploratory trips until they are confident enough to look the whole place over. Then there are other cats, including many Peterbald cats, who will settle pretty quickly so long as their owner is there. Of course there are also cats that will only emerge from hiding after being bribed, cajoled and begged.

Some cat owners find it helpful to go on a tour of the new house with their cat. If your cat is too nervous to follow you or walk with you, you could pick it up and do the tour together. Again, make sure to speak soothingly to your Peterbald and pet him or her so they know all is well.

As a rule, if your furniture is in place and most smells are familiar your cat will settle in well and make the necessary adjustments. If, however, your cat is of a generally more nervous disposition it might not be a bad idea to speak to your vet about a mild sedative to help your Peterbald make the move more easily and with less stress.

Chapter 11: Becoming a Peterbald breeder

If you want to breed Peterbald cats you will need several things in addition to a passion for it: a vet with whom you have a good relationship and who understands and knows the breed, lots of available time, energy, a mentor or advisor such as an established breeder, the ability to deal with some heartache and the necessary money.

If you only want to breed the Peterbald because you have heard there are waiting lists for them and money to be made, you are in the wrong business.

As a breeder you will need to be even more hygiene and health conscious than you are as a cat owner. The kittens especially are vulnerable when they are very young and can be prone to respiratory illnesses. In fact, one of your responsibilities will be to learn about cat illnesses. You need to read a lot, talk to vets and or breeders and get as much information as you can so that you can pick up signs or symptoms early. In other words, a breeder must know about illnesses, transmission, prevention and treatment.

It is also advisable to become a registered breeder. Find out from an internet search, your mentor, an existing breeder or your vet which associations you need to investigate and join. Membership gives you access to really useful information and a support network. It also gives your credibility as a breeder in the eyes of people who will buy kittens from you. There are also numerous very helpful – and often fun – blogs, newsletters, clubs, associations, forums and chat rooms out there that focus on the Peterbald breed. Have a look at them, join or follow them or subscribe to newsletters and decide which you find useful or just enjoyable. It can be very productive to spend time in chat rooms or open blogs where Peterbald breeders and owners share experiences and offer comments or advice.

1) Sexual maturity

If you buy a registered Peterbald kitten with a view to becoming a breeder, you need to know when it is sexually mature and at what age you can start to breed with it.

Both males (toms) and females (queens) usually reach puberty at around 6 months. However, as with humans there are always some variations. Some cats reach sexual maturity as early as 4 months. On the other hand, some females are only ready at about a year. You will have to establish the status of your cat by its behaviour.

A female cat will come onto heat. When she does you will notice that she is far more affectionate and vocal than usual. She may also yowl to attract a mate. You need to keep your very young female inside and safe because you don't want her to get pregnant by a non Peterbald or when she is still too young.

Males that are sexually mature will also become far more vocal. They will try to get out and may also spray to mark territory and attract a female. Here again you need to keep your male cat inside until the urge to mate subsides.

Females should not be used for breeding until they are 18 to 24 months old. Males should not be used until they are 18 months old. You want a cat that is not only sexually mature but also fully grown, strong and more grown up. At the other end of the spectrum, one should not breed with cats that are older than 4 or 5 years.

2) Breeding: general pointers

The single most important activity is monitoring a female's heat cycle very carefully. When a cat is in heat, 1 or 2 eggs are released by the ovaries in a 24 hour period. If your cat's heat lasts 7 days that's 7 to 14 eggs. So, a female cat that mates each of those 7 days could well conceive on each day.

Given a week in a cat pregnancy is like a month for a human one, the kitten(s) conceived on day 7 will be born at the same time as the kitten(s) conceived on day 1. The day 7 kitten is effectively premature and therefore vulnerable to a number of potentially fatal health problems. These premature kittens are often called the "runt of the litter" because they are smaller, less developed and not as strong and robust.

The solution is pretty simple: only allow your female to mate during the first half (2 or 3 days) of the heat cycle. That way all the kittens will be developed to almost identical stages and you will greatly reduce the chance of loosing kittens.

The interval between one heat cycle and another is usually about 10 days. So expect your cat to exhibit this behaviour at least twice in a month during the breeding season.

The hormonal changes that take place in the cat's body in this period are tremendous. While oestrogen causes the onset of the heat cycle, progesterone takes over when she is pregnant. As the level of oestrogen increases, the heat cycle will intensify. Once the level of oestrogen drops, the heat cycle ends. This rise and fall of oestrogen will only end when she is mated.

The mating season usually starts in January or February and continues until October or November. The temperature during this season and the ratio between light and dark hours will play a significant role in your cat's heat cycle.

3) Finding the right mate

Cats are extremely sensitive creatures. Most often, they will be able to choose their own mates when you take them to the breeder. You must always take a queen to the tom for breeding as she will not be too sensitive to these environmental changes during the mating process.

The actual mating does not last for more than 4 minutes. Once this is over, the queen will break free by striking the male with her paw and turning away. The after-reaction of the female is to clean after rolling and thrashing for a while. The after-reaction may last up to 9 minutes.

If you are interested in producing a litter, you may have to allow your cat to be mated multiple times. With a single mating, there is only a 50% chance of your cat getting pregnant. Studies show that female cats will allow up to 30 matings at intervals of 5 minutes.

One interesting fact about cats in general is that while each kitten has one father, the kittens in a single litter may not have the same father. This is true because of the multiple mating processes. Of course this will not be the case if the queen is only covered by one tom.

Once the kittens arrive you also need to make sure both mother and babies are kept at the right temperature. Although the Peterbald has a body temperature that is a couple of degrees higher than other breeds, they feel the cold more… for obvious reasons. You must keep the basket or nesting place out of drafts as the kittens are prone to respiratory problems when they are very little. They aren't able to regulate their body temperature the way the adults can. If they get too cold they can't digest their milk or get the nutrients they need. Using a heating pad or hot water bottle can. Just remember to keep the heat low as the kittens can't get away from it and could overheat as easily as they get too cold.

4) What to feed your pregnant cat

The most important rule is to continue to feed her a healthy and balanced diet. A pregnant cat may ask for extra food but resist her pleas; extra food will result in weight gain which will be bad for her as it puts stress on the organs and therefore on the unborn kittens.

Some vets recommend a diet that contains calcium, phosphorus and extra protein. It's also suggested that several small meals throughout the day is better for a pregnant cat that two larger meals each day.

5) Gestation

For the first 3 to 4 weeks one usually can't tell anything about the cat's condition. You will probably notice behaviour changes first. She will become even more home loving and will probably start to sleep more. A pregnant cat often becomes even more affectionate and demonstrative to its owners and more attention seeking than usual.

In the fourth week the nipples or teats will start to become a darker pink and to protrude. In the fifth week you will notice that her tummy is gradually getting rounder. The standard gestation period for cats is 62 to 65 days. There is certainly some variation by a day or two on either side.

About two weeks, sometimes one, before the kittens are due the mother will begin to look for a suitable place in which to give birth. It's not a bad idea to provide a basket or a box with a towel or blanket in it in a place that is peaceful and warm.

The box or basket must also be of sufficient size to allow the cat to stretch out full length. Of course in typical cat fashion you will know soon enough if what you have provided is not what she wants! Your cat may go off and select a draw or cupboard or somewhere else that is not ideal from your point of view but certainly is from hers.

By the 16th day of pregnancy the rounded abdomen should make it obvious that your cat is pregnant. If you are not experienced with cats, an ultrasound can help you decide if your cat is pregnant or not. There is an easy way to check. If the uterus feels stringy, it means that your cat might be pregnant. By the 20th day of pregnancy, you can actually feel the kitten foetuses in the abdomen of the queen when she is relaxed.

Besides checking for pregnancy, ultrasound is also a useful tool to check if the development of the foetuses is normal. You can have an ultrasound performed from the 26th day of pregnancy until the end of pregnancy.

6) Special care for a pregnant cat

The pregnancy period is a very delicate one. You must ensure that you take the best care of your Peterbald so that she has a healthy litter and a safe delivery. There are a few things to keep in mind while caring for a pregnant cat:

- ✓ Morning sickness is common in cats. Your vet will be able to provide you with assistance if this persists.
- ✓ Your pregnant cat may also reduce her food consumption by the third week of pregnancy.
- ✓ Overfeeding and weight gain during pregnancy can lead to complications during labour.
- ✓ The food that you give your queen must be highly nutritious.
- ✓ Protein and calcium are a must. However, never provide any supplements unless recommended by a vet.
- ✓ Your cat must be kept indoors during the last 15 days of pregnancy. This helps you ensure that she does not give birth elsewhere.
- ✓ During your cat's pregnancy you must make sure that you take her to the vet regularly. The most important time for vet visits is during the last two weeks of pregnancy.

Continue with the usual grooming routine and lavish her with love, affection and praise.

7) Preparing for and assisting at the birth

There are a few things that you should keep in handy when your Peterbald is in the last two weeks of her pregnancy:

- A sturdy box of some sort
- Surgical gloves
- Syringe or eyedropper to remove secretions from the kitten's noses and mouths if necessary.
- Cotton thread or dental floss for the umbilical cord ties
- Antiseptic for the umbilical stumps
- Sharp, clean scissors
- Clean and fresh towels
- The vet's number or emergency contact numbers.

Now, all you need to do is prepare for the actual birth. When your cat is in the last week of her pregnancy, place the kittening box in a quiet spot. This spot should be warm and completely draft free.

Place your cat's favourite blanket and some toys in this box to encourage her to sleep there. The bedding that you choose should be comfortable for the kittens and shouldn't snag their claws. This bedding must be changed regularly after the birth.

Danger signs during pregnancy

If you observe one or more of the following symptoms, you must contact your vet right away:

- Lack of appetite in your queen for 24 hours or more
- Your cat's temperature is high and stays elevated
- She becomes lethargic and lacks interest in anything
- There is an unpleasant smelling discharge from the vagina.

These are all signs that something might have gone wrong and must be treated at the earliest opportunity to care for her and protect the unborn kittens.

Things not to do

- Never use any flea powder or medicine without consulting your doctor first.
- Don't give your Peterbald medication without a valid prescription
- Do not use antiseptics suitable for humans. These products may burn your cat's delicate skin.
- Avoid handling the kittens too much; there is a chance that a cat will disown or even kill her kittens if she feels they are threatened. Allow the kittens and the mother to bond.
- Don't let your cat to roam around. Cats can get pregnant again within 2 weeks of delivery, so keep her confined for a while.
- Have your cat sterilised in the 7 weeks after the kittens' birth.

Taking care of a pregnant cat is a huge responsibility. If you are not sure of how to go about it, you can look for a shelter or a veterinary hospital where the cats will be taken care of till the kittens are born. Once the kittens arrive, you can decide if you want to keep them in your home or find them another loving home.

You will notice that your pregnant cat starts to become rather restless at about 12 or 24 hours before she's going to give birth. She will go back and inspect the nesting place several times, sometimes adjusting the bedding. At this point she will probably also stop eating.

8) The birth itself

The first sign that the birth is imminent is that there will be a slight discharge of clear amniotic fluid; the feline equivalent of water breaking. As with human beings and other animals, contractions will become stronger and closer together as labour progresses. There is no hard and fast rule about how your cat will

Chapter 11: Becoming a Peterbald breeder

behave while she is in labour. Cats with very strong bonds to their humans, like the Peterbald, will probably not want to be left on their own. However, more experienced mothers are quite happy to get on with it on their own in peace and quiet.

Once the cervix has opened, expulsion contractions begin. The cat will usually lie on her side or even squat, using her stomach muscles to assist the contractions. The birth of the kittens occurs rapidly. Most kittens are born headfirst but almost a third of kittens are breech births with the hindquarters appearing first.

When the kitten has been born the mother will tear the amniotic sac open if it hasn't already broken. She will drink the fluid and eat the sac and then begin to lick and clean the kitten. This licking not only cleans and dries the kitten but it also stimulates the newborn's circulation and respiration.

Once all the kittens have been born the placenta is discharged or removed and eaten by the mother. If the umbilical cord has not already detached, the mother will nibble gently through it. The reason the mother disposes of the amniotic sac, fluid and placenta is to keep her nest clean, prevent smells and it also provides her with high quality, energy boosting food.

9) Dealing with the umbilical cord if the mother doesn't

In the unlikely event that the mother does not sever the umbilical cord herself you must do so. It's very important to remember that you need to wait 5 to 10 minutes before severing the cord. If you don't there is a risk that the kitten will suffer brain damage. This is as a result of depriving the kitten of maximum blood supply during the crucial first few minutes after birth.

Before cutting the cord, apply a ligature by tying a piece of thread or dental floss that has been soaked in a disinfectant solution around the umbilical cord about 2 cm (3/4") from the kitten's body. Cut the cord with disinfected scissors 1 cm (1/3") from the ligature on the side of the placenta, not the kitten. Then you need to clean the cut end of the cord with tincture of iodine or some other disinfectant solution.

10) Feeding kittens if the mother can't or shouldn't

Sometimes a kitten has to be hand fed because the mother has died, has no milk, rejects the kitten or the kitten is too weak to suckle.

You can either purchase a kitten formula from your vet or you can make up your own. The first do-it-yourself formula contains 1 cup evaporated or powdered milk mixed with boiled water and made up to double the strength recommended for human babies. Add one egg yolk and 1 teaspoon of glucose additive to the mixture. The second option is to use half a cup of cow's milk mixed with an egg yolk and 1 teaspoon of glucose. If the kitten gets diarrhoea, you need to dilute the mixture further.

Before you begin to feed the kitten make sure that the substitute milk is body temperature. During the first week of life a kitten requires about 5 ml or 1 teaspoon of milk substitute every two hours. Thereafter the frequency of feedings should be decreased and the amount of milk substitute increased. Four hourly feeding is sufficient once the kitten has reached the age of 2 weeks.

There are two methods that can be used to feed the kitten. Firstly one can do bottle feeding. With this method, you should hold the kitten firmly but gently with its head elevated slightly. Move the teat in and out of the mouth and express a small amount of milk to encourage the kitten to develop a sucking response.

If you are dealing with a very small and weak kitten you may need to resort to stomach tube feeding. It is strongly recommended that you consult your local vet for a demonstration of the correct way to do this so that no damage is accidentally done to the oesophagus or any other internal organs or tissue.

Chapter 12: The aging Peterbald cat

1) The aging Peterbald

As with any other species, humans included, aging brings an increasing number of health problems and general deterioration. The aging process can't be stopped, but there are some things we can do to minimise the effects.

Age related changes

The changes you will see in your cat include:

- *Claws*: while some body processes are slowing down, cat's claws actually grow faster as they get older so it is necessary to trim their nails more frequently.

- *Feeding and drinking*: an older cat may experience a loss of appetite or be reluctant to eat. If he or she is experiencing problems with their teeth or gums this could also cause difficulty. Older cats feel thirsty more often than younger cats

- *Digestive problems*: your cat may not be able to process food the way it did or tolerate the same kinds of food. It can be helpful to feed your cat three or four small meals a day, increase the amount of moist foods in the diet or move to special or prescription food. Your vet will be able to advise you about the best one for your Peterbald.

- *Sleep*: aging cats will want and need to sleep even more than their younger counterparts. In addition, their sleep is often deeper and your cat is likely to be very startled if woken suddenly. Wherever possible, allow your elderly feline friend to sleep quietly and undisturbed.

- *Weight loss*: this often occurs gradually - over a period of several months - and you might not notice at first. The weight loss occurs even when the cat continues to eat well.

- *Joint changes*: arthritis and osteoarthritis will cause your cat to move stiffly when he or she first gets or wakes up. In more advanced stages, a cat may have difficulty walking and jumping up onto surfaces such as beds and chairs. As soon as you notice these symptoms in your Peterbald, take him or her to the vet for treatment or at least symptomatic and pain relief.

- *Constipation*: if your cat is an outdoors cat, you may not notice that he or she is having this difficulty. It is important, however, not to allow this to continue as it could result in a potentially dangerous bowel blockage or obstruction. Cat laxative products are available from vets.

- *Blindness*: usually a cat's eye sight will deteriorate gradually. Signs to look out for are white patches near the centre of the eye or a bluish, slightly opaque film over the eye. Once the cat's eyesight has become really bad you will notice him or her starting to walk into furniture and show reluctance to go out. All you can do is take steps to protect your cat from obvious dangers like stairs and pools and not change the environment, for instance don't move furniture around.

- *Deafness*: like failing eyesight, loss of hearing also usually happens over an extended period of time. It may take a while for you to notice that your Peterbald does not respond to noises or to being called. This makes them more at risk if they are outdoors as they won't hear other animals or cars approaching.

- *Senility*: if your cat suffers from this condition you will notice that he or she will seem particularly restless and disorientated. There may also be increased meowing or crying and a greater demand for your attention as your cat seeks comfort and reassurance. In other words, even your Peterbald will want more attention than usual and need to be comforted and reassured. You need to be patient, loving and understanding and involve your vet as and when necessary.

2) *How to make your aging Peterbald more comfortable*

While you can do very little about some of the symptoms and problems your cat will face, there are certain things you can do to reduce your cat's discomfort and stress.

Firstly, monitor your cat's food and drink intake. If necessary, heat your cat's food slightly to encourage it to eat. Alternatively, introduce something new into the diet. If your cat is being very inactive and sleeping a great deal you need to decrease its food intake slightly. If you don't, he or she will put on weight and this can lead to other health problems. Also, if possible, be aware of bowel activity and urination.

Secondly, place your cat's bed and bedding in a quiet spot that is out of direct sun and drafts and close to the litter box if your Peterbald is using one.

Next, you should accompany your elderly cat into outdoor areas or other places where he or she may encounter difficulties or dangers, especially if your cat has poor vision and or hearing.

Finally, take your cat to the vet for regular check-ups and monitoring. You need to maintain vaccinations and all the standard health and hygiene routines.

3) *How do you know it's time to let go?*

One response to this question that struck a cord is that it is time to say goodbye to your elderly Peterbald companion when he or she no longer responds to you and seems to get no pleasure from life. Certainly nobody wants to see a creature they love suffering or fading away.

The Downing Centre for Animal Pain Management drew up a scale to measure animal's quality of life. The test itself was developed by a veterinary oncologist. The criteria the test uses are: pain levels, the ability to eat enough to prevent hunger or malnutrition, the ability to drink and stay hydrated, the ability to groom or be groomed and the cat's ability to move around or be mobile. In other words, the scale looks at pain levels, appetite and the ability to eat, the ability to drink, whether the cat can still groom itself, if there is evidence that the cat can still enjoy activities and interactions with people and other animals, that he or she can walk or move around with relative ease and, finally, if the cat has more days that are good than ones that are bad.

Each criterion should be rated on a scale of 1 to 10 with 10 being ideal, for example pain-free would be 10. If your cat scores more than 35 then its quality of life is still acceptable. A score below that and you need to start considering euthanasia.

Chapter 13: Prices and costs

1) How to choose a breeder

Taking the time to do some research to find good and reputable Peterbald breeders is well worth it. A good place to start is with cat registries such as TICA or CFA. The various cat associations also offer breeder lists on their websites. In fact, the more investigating you do and the more people you talk to the better.

In addition to being able to find breeders details on the Internet, you will also be able to locate the "bad breeder list". Knowing which breeder not to go to is as useful as knowing which ones to approach. You could also join Peterbald forums online and follow or contribute to blogs. Chatting to Peterbald owners could also provide you with very valuable information.

How do you recognize a reputable breeder? There is no way of choosing a breeder that is 100% safe, but there are some things that you can look out for. A reputable breeder:

- Will be able to show you references and proof of registration
- Won't sell kittens younger than 12 weeks old
- Will show you around his or her facility
- Won't have multiple litters available at the same time
- Will be able to provide proof of vaccinations and so on
- Won't sell kittens to pet stores
- Will breed using pedigreed cats and can prove it
- Won't sell kittens for a far lower price than the average
- Will offer a health guarantee on kittens.

Taking time to select the right breeder is a crucial first step in finding a healthy Peterbald that is right for you. Don't rush the process or you could regret doing so later.

Chapter 13: Prices and costs

2) The cost to purchase a Peterbald cat or kitten

The price of Peterbald kittens varies from breeder to breeder, country to country. Even within countries there can be regional differences.

At time of writing, the price range was considerable. Some breeders charge $500 (£290) per kitten and those that sell highly pedigreed kittens can sell for as much as $1400 (£865).

Although it is unlikely, a Peterbald kitten might be found at a shelter. Some adult cats are offered for rehoming by breeders too. In these situations the price will be less.

A word of caution: if you see kittens advertised for less than $500 (£290) each they are probably the products of 'kitten mills' and should be avoided. The so-called breeder should be reported to your local cat or Peterbald association and an animal welfare organization.

3) Monthly costs of caring for your cat

Monthly costs will clearly be determined by a wide range of factors including your location, your choice of brands and products, your kitten or cat's age and its state of health. If you own a Peterbald you need to be able to accommodate the following regular expenses:

- ✓ Good quality cat food
- ✓ Grooming products
- ✓ Vaccination and deworming costs
- ✓ Cat litter
- ✓ Toys
- ✓ Food and water bowls
- ✓ Treats
- ✓ (Sometimes high) vet bills following illness or injury
- ✓ Pet insurance (optional).

Once-off expenses will include registration (if necessary), having your Peterbald spayed or neutered, micro-chipping and a cat carrier. These once-off costs, at time of writing, were in the region of:

- A litter box: $3-20 / £3-28
- Carrier: $20-50 / £15-45
- Toys: average $3 / £2.50 each
- Food and water bowls: $4-10 / £1-10
- Scratch post: $ / £4-110

There are also items that will have to be replaced from time to time such as beds and bedding, scratching posts, toys and food and water bowls.

Monthly costs were:

- Food: $17 / £15
- Cat litter: $10 / £12
- Grooming and flea control: $10 / £8
- Vet: $28 / £32 (based on vaccines and annual check-up) Total: $65 / £67

Owning a pet is a big financial responsibility. It is as good as having a baby at home. If you think that you might have to compromise on any of the expenses mentioned above, you need to re-think your decision of bringing home a cat. Having a Peterbald will involve costs but everybody who owns one of these cats feels that it is money well spent.

4) The option to take out Pet Insurance

If you give your Peterbald the right diet, perform all the necessary grooming and dental care and get vaccinations and deworming done as and when required, your cat should stay pretty healthy. Of course, no cat is completely safe from illness and even the healthiest cat can be injured. Cats are also living longer now and so they suffer from illnesses associated with age. In addition, vet care is becoming more expensive.

Enter pet insurance. Depending on where you are you may be able to opt to take out one of several types of cover to help you with bills when your cat needs medical care. Some insurers offer the choice of a plan that covers expenses in the event of an accident only. Others will pay costs for both accident and illness. The third option, one that usually gets added onto one of the others, is to cover routine medical costs such as vaccinations, deworming, dental descaling and sterilisations.

Like most insurance, most of these policies will have a deductible or excess that you will have to pay, but they can help greatly if your Peterbald ever requires significant or ongoing treatment or vet care. The premium and affordability will also vary depending on the type of cover chosen and how many pets you place on the policy.

Your vet should be able to supply you with a brochure, pamphlet or information. You will have to weigh the cost of insurance against the possibility of being out of pocket at a later date.

Chapter 14: General advice & tips

Mistakes made by new Peterbald owners

If you have just got yourself a Peterbald cat you must make its maintenance and safety your priority. When you bring home a new cat, you get so caught up in settling it in and then playing with and petting it that you can loose sight of some important aspects. There are in fact several mistakes that new cat owners make.

If you take cat care too lightly, there is a chance that your cat will not be happy and satisfied in your home. Here are some of the most concerning mistakes a Peterbald owner could make:

Underestimating the cost of owning a cat

Of course, bringing home a cat is not as expensive as bringing home a dog. This, however, does not mean that it is easy to have a cat at home. The expenses of taking care of the cat, its health and also the facilities that it requires can be quite a bit. In addition to that, cats are a big responsibility. You will have to think twice before you plan a vacation or holiday. You will have to plan your entire schedule around your Peterbald. If you are unable or unwilling to do that, owning a cat can be a serious problem for you.

Ignoring visits to the vet

You must make sure that you make a schedule of all the necessary visits to the vet. If you neglect to do so, there is a good chance that your cat may not get the necessary vaccinations on time or at all. In addition, you might not notice the symptoms and signs of potentially hazardous diseases. Going to the vet will also help you understand if your routine with your cat is correct or not. In case you need to make changes in the diet or the amount of exercise

Chapter 14: General advice & tips

that your cat gets, your vet can provide you with the assistance you require before problems occur.

Failure to spay or neuter your Peterbald

Breeding or mating is not the easiest thing to do with cats. In case you have ignored spaying or neutering, you will find your home in a mess during the time that your cat is in heat. It is common for male Peterbald cats to want to roam. Female cats, on the other hand, will keep the entire household on their feet with constant purring and yowling when she is in heat.

Given that the Peterbald purr is loud and shrill, you do not want to find yourself in this situation. The worst thing that can happen to you is a litter of kittens when you are not prepared for one. Being unable to care for a pregnant cat or the kittens can be very stressful for you and your cat.

Buying cheap cat food

If you try to save money on cat food remember that you will probably end up paying much more later to help your cat recover from nutrition and health related issues. Remember that your cat food must be a good source of proteins. If you are unable to do that, your Peterbald will be malnourished and unhealthy.

Cheaper varieties of cat food will probably only be able to provide your cat with plant based proteins or inferior forms of meat. For an animal that is a carnivore the only good source of protein is animal protein. In addition to this, cheap foods also contain high amounts of carbohydrates that can make your cat obese or diabetic. Make sure you only feed your cat age appropriate and high quality foods that supply all the necessary nutrients, proteins, fats and vitamins.

Allowing your cat to roam outside

By nature, a Peterbald likes to stay indoors. If you let it loose outside there are chances that he or she will consume food that is poisonous or hazardous to his health. Your cat may also be attacked by bigger animals and get infected. Domesticated cats are not aggressive or defensive enough to take care of themselves in the great outdoors. In addition, the Peterbald is far more vulnerable to sun burn and cold than the majority of cats.

Neglecting litter box hygiene

Cats are very fussy about hygiene. If you do not clean the litter box regularly, you will notice peculiar behaviour patterns like littering in other places inside the house. Some cats will also not eat well if the litter box hygiene is not maintained appropriately. Examine the litter box regularly and ensure that the litter is replaced on a regular basis. A dirty litter box also poses health risks to the human family members.

Thinking your Peterbald is a human being

No matter how intelligent, loving, funny and so on your cat is she or he is… a cat. Conversely, your cat may well view you as a large not terribly athletic cat. This means that you have to try and view things from your cat's point of view. Your cat will have a reason for the things it does. It's part of the cat owner's job to work out what those reasons are.

Hitting your Peterbald

Don't hit your cat, ever. There is never anything positive to be gained from this. Although they are intelligent creatures, you can't be sure that your cat will know why it is being smacked. The result you are likely to have is a cat that becomes fearful of you and anxious. If you need to discipline your cat, do so when you catch it 'in the act'. You can clap your hands, use a firm tone when saying "No" or even spray the cat lightly with water.

Conclusion

The Peterbald is a unique creature. This cat is elegant, intelligent, affectionate, playful and loving. It is a true extrovert that demands attention and will be miserable if it is ignored. The Peterbald also gets on well with other animals, both cat-friendly dogs and cats, and with children.

This high energy cat can perform acrobatic tricks and is skilled at balancing and climbing. They love to be entertained and to entertain. The Peterbald will clown around and show off.

These cats are also curious and mischievous, and these qualities, coupled with the high level of intelligence found in this breed, can make it a handful. But, it is also a sweet-natured, well behaved and easy to handle breed. It will be a doting, loyal and entertaining companion to you for many years in the normal course of events.

Balanced against these numerous advantages is the fact that the Peterbald is also time consuming and energy intensive. If you own one of these cats you must spend time on grooming, cuddling and playing. If you can't do this, or are not prepared to do so, don't get a Peterbald.

In other words, if you want a cat that is docile, quiet and low maintenance the Peterbald is definitely not for you. If, on the other hand, you want a cat that is smart, funny, boisterous and doting then there is no better breed!

If you already have a Peterbald in your life I hope you have gained some useful new information and insights. If you were undecided about the breed I hope you are closer to a decision. If you are going to buy a Peterbald, I trust the information here helps to prepare you.

Here is a final checklist to make sure you do not miss anything.

Conclusion

- Keep an eye on your pet. You don't have to become an obsessive parent. However, you must be sensitive to changes in your cat both physically and mentally.
- Adapt your home accordingly so that your Peterbald never feels threatened.
- Grooming time is mandatory for a cat like the Peterbald. If you ignore this important part of taking care of it, chances are that your cat will develop skin and other health problems. You may also get oily patches on your furniture and clothes.
- Treat him or her like the centre of your universe. The Peterbald is not forgiving if it is ignored or neglected and will become stressed or even depressed.
- Make time to play: If your work comes first, do not even try to tell your Peterbald that. They do not understand how you could possibly be too busy to play with them. Involve yourself in their playtime or you will find almost incessant meowing demolishing any chance of peace and quiet.
- Feed him or her well: Your cat is domesticated. It does not know to hunt for prey. You must keep a schedule and make sure that someone is always around to feed your cat on time. Unlike humans who would eat just about anything at any time of the day, cats are highly disciplined creatures.
- Get all the necessary identification to ensure that your Peterbald does not end up in a shelter. Consider having your cat micro-chipped but, at the very least, get a tear-away collar with an identification disc
- Your cat's health is priority. No matter how tired or lazy you feel, you need to make sure you take your pet to the vet at the scheduled times for vaccinations, deworming, etc. Any negligence in this area can have serious and really expensive repercussions for your Peterbald and for you.

Savour every minute of being the proud owner of a Peterbald. You have a companion who will love you as long as he or she lives. Your Peterbald will be a doting, loyal and entertaining companion for many years in the normal course of events.

Published by IMB Publishing 2014

Copyright and Trademarks: This publication is Copyrighted 2014 by IMB Publishing. All products, publications, software and services mentioned and recommended in this publication are protected by trademarks. In such instance, all trademarks & copyright belong to the respective owners. All rights reserved. No part of this book may be reproduced or transferred in any form or by any means, graphic, electronic, or mechanical, including photocopying, recording, taping, or by any information storage retrieval system, without the written permission of the authors. Pictures used in this book are either royalty free pictures bought from stock-photo websites or have the source mentioned underneath the picture.

Disclaimer and Legal Notice: This product is not legal or medical advice and should not be interpreted in that manner. You need to do your own due-diligence to determine if the content of this product is right for you. The author and the affiliates of this product are not liable for any damages or losses associated with the content in this product. While every attempt has been made to verify the information shared in this publication, neither the author nor the affiliates assume any responsibility for errors, omissions or contrary interpretation of the subject matter herein. Any perceived slights to any specific person(s) or organization(s) are purely unintentional. We have no control over the nature, content and availability of the web sites listed in this book. The inclusion of any web site links does not necessarily imply a recommendation or endorse the views expressed within them. IMB Publishing takes no responsibility for, and will not be liable for, the websites being temporarily unavailable or being removed from the Internet. The accuracy and completeness of information provided herein and opinions stated herein are not guaranteed or warranted to produce any particular results, and the advice and strategies, contained herein may not be suitable for every individual. The author shall not be liable for any loss incurred as a consequence of the use and application, directly or indirectly, of any information presented in this work. This publication is designed to provide information in regards to the subject matter covered. The information included in this book has been compiled to give an overview of the subject s and detail some of the symptoms, treatments etc. that are available to people with this condition. It is not intended to give medical advice. For a firm diagnosis of your condition, and for a treatment plan suitable for you, you should consult your doctor or consultant. The writer of this book and the publisher are not responsible for any damages or negative consequences following any of the treatments or methods highlighted in this book. Website links are for informational purposes and should not be seen as a personal endorsement; the same applies to the products detailed in this book. The reader should also be aware that although the web links included were correct at the time of writing, they may become out of date in the future.

www.ingramcontent.com/pod-product-compliance
Lightning Source LLC
Chambersburg PA
CBHW060836050426
42453CB00008B/710